WITHDRAWN

Authentic Ethnographic Research in the Classroom

EXPLORING
People
&Cultures

T0204743

Authentic Ethnographic Research in the Classroom

EXPLORING

People & Cultures

Help Kids Learn About Culture Through Challenging Research Activities

by Mary Ellen Sweeney, Ph.D., and Brooke Walker, Ph.D.

PRUFROCK PRESS INC.
WACO, TEXAS

Copyright ©2012 Prufrock Press Inc.

Edited by Lacy Compton

Production design by Raquel Trevino

ISBN-13: 978-1-59363-957-0

The purchase of this book entitles the buyer to reproduce student activity pages for single classroom use only. Other use requires written permission of publisher. All rights reserved.

At the time of this book's publication, all facts and figures cited are the most current available; all telephone numbers, addresses, and website URLs are accurate and active; all publications, organizations, websites, and other resources exist as described in this book; and all have been verified. The authors and Prufrock Press make no warranty or guarantee concerning the information and materials given out by organizations or content found at websites, and we are not responsible for any changes that occur after this book's publication. If you find an error or believe that a resource listed here is not as described, please contact Prufrock Press.

Prufrock Press Inc.
P.O. Box 8813
Waco, TX 76714-8813
Phone: (800) 998-2208
Fax: (800) 240-0333
http://www.prufrock.com

Table of Contents

Introduction

Ethnographic Research

> *The ethnographer is both storyteller and scientist; the closer the reader of an ethnography comes to understanding the native's point of view, the better the story and the better the science.*
>
> — Fetterman (1989, p. 12)

What Is Ethnography?

Ethnography is a branch of cultural anthropology. An ethnographer is an anthropologist who becomes immersed in a culture to observe, record, and describe its culturally significant behaviors (Flake, 1992). The description may be of a small tribal group in some exotic land or a classroom in a middle-American city (Fetterman, 1989; Walker, 2000). Ethnographic research requires a period of study in a well-defined community, good observational techniques, face-to-face interviews with informants, and participation in group activities.

The ethnographer uses the scientific research design of posing a question, gathering data, analyzing data, and drawing conclusions based on those data. However, the ethnographer goes beyond these steps to entertain alternative interpretations of data throughout the study. Rather than looking at a small set of variables and a large number of subjects ("the big picture"), the ethnographer attempts to get a detailed understanding of the circumstances of the few subjects being studied (Agar, 1986; Fetterman, 1989). Ethnographic accounts are both descriptive and interpretive: descriptive because the ethnographer illustrates what he observes to the reader, and interpretive because the ethnographer must interpret what he describes to unravel the meaning for the reader. Let's revisit the opening quote to understand the significance of both description and interpretation: "The ethnographer is both storyteller and scientist; the closer the reader of an ethnography comes to understanding the native's point of view, the better the story and the better the science" (Fetterman, 1989, p. 12).

Why Teach Ethnographic Research?

Ethnographic skills benefit students who are living in complex educational, urban, suburban, or rural settings. Learning ethnographic skills will help students adapt to a variety of social circumstances, as their intrapersonal skills will be enhanced. Intrapersonal skills are a challenge for many gifted and high-achieving students and adults who will be involved in professional and other work efforts as future workers on teams or in departments. Ethnographic research skills will behoove gifted students in all employment paths. Through the acquisition of ethnographic skills, adolescents' educational efforts and workplace pursuits will be enhanced.

The teaching of ethnography allows the teacher to capitalize on the research regarding effective teaching and learning, as it provides opportunities for:

✦ the integration of subject areas;
✦ the use of complex, real-world projects and experiences;
✦ the development of creativity in students; and
✦ the use of computer applications to demonstrate and apply learning.

The teaching of these skills will give gifted and advanced students a clearer understanding of patterns of human behaviors. Gifted students will be more apt to work cooperatively in future group, educational, and work endeavors.

Research shows that the most effective learning occurs when students are immersed in a study and when connections are made among the various subject areas under study (Caine & Caine, 1991; Marzano, 1992). Integrated curriculum facilitates the accommodation of new information by building on the students' knowledge base. The learning experiences become more meaningful as students connect their learning to prior understandings. The study of ethnography allows students to do this, as it will include strands from language arts, science, social studies, and math. The scientific method is included, as it is used to generate research questions, gather and analyze data, and then draw and report on conclusions. Using their language arts skills, students develop final research reports that are both persuasive and appropriate for the intended audience. Surveys and sampling employ mathematical methods.

Both real experiences and projects are important elements in facilitating students' learning (Caine & Caine, 1991; Piaget, 1954; Vygotsky, 1978). Through ethnography, students will be exposed to subject matter by multiple methods through complex, real-world projects and experiences. Throughout the study, students will be involved in observing and writing about familiar and novel settings in their own communities. In the first stage of the study, students will learn about and apply beginning field observation methods to an actual setting to be identified by them, such as a skate park or a bike shop. In the second stage, students will undertake their own ethnographic studies.

Creativity, deemed an important characteristic for students to develop as they become adults in our quickly changing world, is infused throughout the study of ethnography in the design and use of innovative ways of gathering and analyzing data, in drawing conclusions, and in writing up those conclusions in both interesting and arresting manners. As noted in the previous section, the ethnographer is both a scientist and a storyteller.

Our complex and diverse society mandates that students need to understand the dynamics of groups and the perspectives of others. In learning about ethnography, students will apply cultural anthropological research methods to understand their own perspectives and those of different cultures and groups. Students in grades 5–8 will transition into many new experiences and groups as they mature, including middle school, secondary school, and beyond. The research skills learned in and through ethnography will heighten students' awareness of identifiable cultural patterns and norms. Ethnography allows for the integration of subject areas; the use of complex, real-world projects and experiences; and the development of creativity in students. Studying ethnography provides teachers with an opportunity to address many learning needs and student interests, as they will use research-based methods of effective teaching and learning.

Ethnography and the Gifted Student

Gifted students require curriculum that enables them to operate both cognitively and affectively at complex levels of thought and feeling (VanTassel-Baska et al., 1988). Studying ethnography allows students to engage in both of these modes.

Students studying ethnographic research are working cognitively at complex and in-depth levels. First, students study a culture in depth by observing, recording, and describing culturally significant behaviors. In looking at the world from an ethnographic perspective, the students will be challenged to make not only the strange familiar but also the familiar strange (Fetterman, 1989). Next, students analyze these complex behaviors to interpret the meaning of their findings. Finally, students synthesize and report this meaning in novel ways by using their personal insights and the perspective of the culture under study to report their findings.

The early research of Leta Hollingsworth indicated that gifted children have social and emotional needs meriting attention (Colangelo & Davis, 1991). Ethnography provides a vehicle for discussing gifted and talented (GT) students' perspectives and the viewpoints of other students, as well as providing opportunities for discussing stereotypes and biases. Some gifted students have atypical social behaviors that would be positively impacted by developing the ability to interpret the behavioral patterns of groups. Completing an ethnography affords students the chance to study interpersonal relationships while investigating different cultural attitudes, beliefs, and values (Agar, 1996). Ethnographic research permits high levels of discussion around these topics.

Table 1, Ethnographic Research: Essential Questions, will give teachers a summary of the essential questions (Wiggins & McTighe, 1998) that guide ethnographic research. What students will know, understand, and be able to do are included on the chart for quick reference.

Summary of Addressed Content Skills

The 31 lessons contained in this book will provide students the opportunity to apply content skills in the areas of math, reading, writing, science, and social studies. This book is designed primarily for students in grades 5–8, although it may be adapted for other ages. The following content skills are based on the Texas Education Agency's (2012) Texas Essential Knowledge and Skills standards for middle school. They align closely with the national standards. They are listed by subject area beginning on page 6. The letters and numbers denote the different knowledge and skills in each subject area.

Table 1
Ethnographic Research: Essential Questions

Essential Questions to Guide Exploration	• How may research be utilized to understand different subcultures? • How is ethnographic research valuable to a student's present and future life skills development?
What Students Will Know	• Facts and information. • Research is a tool to learn about the world and its inhabitants. • Social science research helps students learn about human behavior. • Ethnographic research describes a culture to others in a way that makes sense. • An ethnographer gathers information through surveys, interviews, document analysis, and field observations. • As researchers, students will propose a question that will guide their studies. • Ethnographers identify and describe patterns, symbols, and other subcultural traits. • Ethnographic vocabulary (see Chapter 1, Lesson 2, and Appendix A).
What Students Will Understand	• Ethnographic research is a life skill that will help students understand cultural traits. • Students will understand how to better immerse themselves into future subcultural groups (e.g., middle school, high school, trade school, college, present and future work groups, extracurricular groups) with an awareness of ethnographic research.
What Students Will Be Able to Do	• Understand and apply the principles and processes of ethnographic research. • Pose a research question and then develop and implement their own research proposal. • Identify the patterns and themes of a subculture. • Analyze and interpret findings from observed, gathered, and analyzed data. • Write and submit a timely mini-ethnography. • Demonstrate a component of the mini-ethnography in a student-organized ethnographic fair. • Make decisions and solve problems. • Increase their appreciation of the diversity of people, subcultures, and languages.

Texas Essential Knowledge and Skills for English Language Arts and Reading (Grade 8):

(10) *Comprehension of Informational Text/Expository Text.* Students analyze, make inferences and draw conclusions about expository text and provide evidence from text to support their understanding.

(12) *Comprehension of Informational Text/Procedural Texts.* Students understand how to glean and use information in procedural texts and documents.

(14) *Writing/Writing Process.* Students use elements of the writing process (planning, drafting, revising, editing, and publishing) to compose text. Students are expected to:

    (A) plan a first draft by selecting a genre appropriate for conveying the intended meaning to an audience, determining appropriate topics through a range of strategies (e.g., discussion, background reading, personal interests, interviews), and developing a thesis or controlling idea;

    (B) develop drafts by choosing an appropriate organizational strategy (e.g., sequence of events, cause-effect, compare-contrast) and building on ideas to create a focused, organized, and coherent piece of writing;

    (C) revise drafts to clarify meaning, enhance style, include simple and compound sentences, and improve transitions by adding, deleting, combining, and rearranging sentences or larger units of text after rethinking how well questions of purpose, audience, and genre have been addressed;

    (D) edit drafts for grammar, mechanics, and spelling; and

    (E) revise final draft in response to feedback from peers and teacher and publish written work for appropriate audiences.

Texas Essential Knowledge and Skills for Science (Grade 8):

    (A) *Scientific investigation and reasoning.*

        (ii) Scientific investigations are conducted for different reasons. All investigations require a research question, careful observations, data gathering, and analysis of the data to identify the patterns that will explain the findings. Descriptive investigations are used to explore new phenomena such as conducting surveys of organisms or measuring the abiotic components in a given habitat. Descriptive statistics include frequency, range, mean, median, and mode. A hypothesis is not required in a descriptive investigation. On the other hand, when conditions can be controlled in order to focus on a single variable, experimental research design is used to determine causation. Students should experience both types of investigations and understand that different scientific research questions require different research designs.

Texas Essential Knowledge and Skills for Social Studies (Grade 8):

(31) *Social studies skills.* The student uses problem-solving and decision-making skills, working independently and with others, in a variety of settings. The student is expected to:

(A) use a problem-solving process to identify a problem, gather information, list and consider options, consider advantages and disadvantages, choose and implement a solution, and evaluate the effectiveness of the solution; and

(B) use a decision-making process to identify a situation that requires a decision, gather information, identify options, predict consequences, and take action to implement a decision.

Texas Essential Knowledge and Skills for Mathematics (Grade 6):

(11) *Underlying processes and mathematical tools.* The student applies Grade 6 mathematics to solve problems connected to everyday experiences, investigations in other disciplines, and activities in and outside of school. The student is expected to:

(A) identify and apply mathematics to everyday experiences, to activities in and outside of school, with other disciplines, and with other mathematical topics;

(B) use a problem-solving model that incorporates understanding the problem, making a plan, carrying out the plan, and evaluating the solution for reasonableness;

(C) select or develop an appropriate problem-solving strategy from a variety of different types, including drawing a picture, looking for a pattern, systematic guessing and checking, acting it out, making a table, working a simpler problem, or working backwards to solve a problem; and

(D) select tools such as real objects, manipulatives, paper/pencil, and technology or techniques such as mental math, estimation, and number sense to solve problems.

Texas Essential Knowledge and Skills for Mathematics (Grade 7):

(13) *Underlying processes and mathematical tools.* The student applies Grade 7 mathematics to solve problems connected to everyday experiences, investigations in other disciplines, and activities in and outside of school. The student is expected to:

(A) identify and apply mathematics to everyday experiences, to activities in and outside of school, with other disciplines, and with other mathematical topics;

(B) use a problem-solving model that incorporates understanding the problem, making a plan, carrying out the plan, and evaluating the solution for reasonableness;

(C) select or develop an appropriate problem-solving strategy from a variety of different types, including drawing a picture, looking for a pattern, systematic guessing and checking, acting it out, making a table, working a simpler problem, or working backwards to solve a problem; and

(D) select tools such as real objects, manipulatives, paper/pencil, and technology or techniques such as mental math, estimation, and number sense to solve problems.

Texas Essential Knowledge and Skills for Mathematics (Grade 8):

(14) *Underlying processes and mathematical tools.* The student applies Grade 8 mathematics to solve problems connected to everyday experiences, investigations in other disciplines, and activities in and outside of school. The student is expected to:

(A) identify and apply mathematics to everyday experiences, to activities in and outside of school, with other disciplines, and with other mathematical topics;

(B) use a problem-solving model that incorporates understanding the problem, making a plan, carrying out the plan, and evaluating the solution for reasonableness;

(C) select or develop an appropriate problem-solving strategy from a variety of different types, including drawing a picture, looking for a pattern, systematic guessing and checking, acting it out, making a table, working a simpler problem, or working backwards to solve a problem; and

(D) select tools such as real objects, manipulatives, paper/pencil, and technology or techniques such as mental math, estimation, and number sense to solve problems. (Texas Education Agency, 2012)

Student ethnographers will also be practicing and developing the following 21st-century learning skills supported by the Association for Supervision and Curriculum Development (ASCD) in a 2008 position statement:

+ acquire and apply core knowledge and critical thinking skill sets;
+ demonstrate creativity, innovation, and flexibility;
+ make decisions and solve problems;
+ use technology to gather, analyze, and synthesize information; and
+ value and appreciate diversity of people, cultures, and languages.

Students will apply and practice the numerous academic and social skills, listed previously, necessary for success for present and future cooperative endeavors. The interdisciplinary web in Figure 1 displays

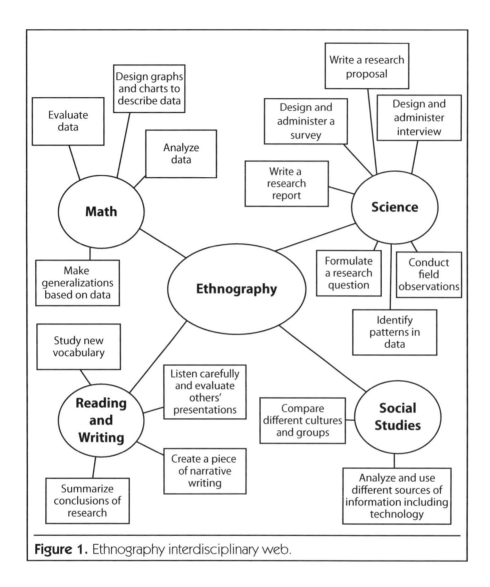

Figure 1. Ethnography interdisciplinary web.

how the different skill and content areas will be addressed in the study of ethnographic research.

The Organization of the Book

The importance of ethnographic skill development for youth was discussed earlier in the Introduction. In Chapter 1, the study of ethnographic research starts with the organization of a research notebook, with beginning lessons to practice data gathering. Students experience ethnographic research processes through applied lessons. Familiarity with ethnographic vocabulary begins in the lessons in Chapter 1 as well. The elements of culture are introduced in Chapter 2. Students will gain and apply insight into their personal and family subcultures. In Chapters 3 and 4, student ethnographers (under the direction of an astute teacher) will brainstorm, implement, analyze, and complete a mini-ethnography of their choosing. The ethnographic research experiences presented in these chapters promise to develop observation skills that will transform the student's cultural perspective in the present and future. In Chapter 5, students will plan a demonstration fair to display, share, and explain their ethnographies and newfound discoveries. Students may elect to guide the demonstration fair's audience through mini-ethnographic research activities, like mapping out a community. Students will be engaged in technology applications throughout the study. In Chapter 1, students will begin to learn the process of ethnographic research through a series of lessons and activities. Students will practice taking field notes, conducting interviews, and analyzing data. We hope you are ready and excited to begin the ethnographic research process in your classroom!

Chapter 1

Ethnographic Research Basics

Research is a scientific process that assumes that events in the world are lawful and orderly and, furthermore, that the lawfulness is discoverable.

—Anderson (1990, p. 5)

The Research Notebook

Students will keep an ongoing research notebook during this unit. The research notebook will be a collection of items the students gather including field notes, interview transcripts, drafts and final papers, reflections on the process, artifacts, articles, and photos. Students will keep all of their work during this unit in their research notebooks in four sections: Section 1 contains the work from Chapter 1, Ethnographic Research Basics; Section 2 contains the work from Chapter 2, A Student Ethnographer's Understanding of the Elements of Culture; Section 3 contains the work from Chapter 3, Student Mini-Ethnographic Proposal; and Section 4 contains the work from Chapter 4, Completing the Mini-Ethnography. See Figure 2 for a sample table of contents for the student research notebook.

As an ethnographer's data are descriptive, the collected data may be voluminous; therefore, ethnographers need to be very organized. A three-ring binder works best for students' research notebooks. A three-hole punch will be needed to allow students to organize their papers in the binder.

Research Notebook Table of Contents

Section 1

Vocabulary	Page	_____
Survey Data		_____
Interview Data		_____
Observation Data		_____
Transcribed Field Notes		_____
Data Analysis		_____
Summary of Results		_____

Section 2

Step In/Step Out	_____
Synthesis of Personal Culture	_____
Bias Essay	_____
Field Notes	_____

Section 3

Brainstorming Web	_____
Topic Browsing Planner	_____
Resources	_____
Research Proposal	_____

Section 4

Interview Transcripts	_____
Field Notes	_____
Research Notes	_____
Rough Draft of Project	_____
Final Project	_____
Completed KWL	_____

Figure 2. Sample research notebook table of contents.

One way to incorporate technology into this unit is to have the teacher and students create a blog or other electronic information sharing site. Blogs can be set up using template sites like http://www.blogger.com. Blogger offers an easy way for the students to share their thoughts with the teacher and each other. Discussion questions could be asked and answered in a blog.

Data-Gathering Practice

Lesson 1 assesses the knowledge that students already have about ethnography and research through a KWL. If students already have a lot of knowledge about research, then some of the lessons in this first chapter could be eliminated. Lesson 2 introduces students to the vocabulary words they will need to learn as they proceed through the study. Some ideas for practicing these vocabulary words are also included in this lesson.

One of the purposes of research in the social sciences is to obtain knowledge about a defined population (e.g., all brown-eyed 10-year-old girls). It's difficult to collect data from all individuals who make up a population. Researchers often select a certain number of subjects to research, called a sample, and then make generalizations about the population from the results of the sample. Lesson 3 introduces students to the idea of making generalizations from a sample.

A method used by researchers who study people (called social scientists) is the survey. The researcher gathers data from a sample so that inferences may be made about some characteristic, attitude, or behavior of this population (Babbie, 1990). The Gallup Poll is probably the best-known survey used to sample public opinion. Have students provide examples of surveys they have heard about or conducted to open a discussion of surveys. Lesson 4 helps students learn to design and complete their own surveys.

Interviews are another way that social scientists collect data. In interviews, researchers obtain responses to questions orally. Interviews differ from surveys because the researcher may modify the data collection to fit the respondent's replies. For example, additional information can be requested or a question may be rephrased (Hittleman & Simon, 1992). An interview may also be used to elicit more in-depth data about information obtained in a survey. The data obtained in an interview are descriptive. Descriptive research is used to illustrate respondents' attitudes, characteristics, and behaviors; therefore, it adds to the knowledge base about a population. Descriptive data are not generalizable to a larger population, however. Lesson 5 takes students through the process of an interview.

Another way that social scientists gather information is by observation. Rather than trying to look at a large population through a few samples, observational data investigate individuals or subjects. Observational research attempts to get a detailed understanding of the few subjects being studied. This method is called fieldwork. Researchers go out into the field, entering a natural setting where they will observe interactions and behaviors. Similar to the interview, this type of research is descriptive; generalizations about a larger population cannot be made from observations. The students will only be able to describe for others what they observe. Observation is the main method of ethnographic research. Ethnographic accounts are descriptive and interpretive. The researcher records observations with as much detail as possible to provide the reader an accurate presentation of the observation site. After presenting the description, the research explains the significance of the data for the reader.

Initial observation research may be approached in several ways. The class could take a field trip to a museum, the zoo, a park, or any place that students might be able to observe people going about their daily business. Students could observe other classes in the building; alternatively, this assignment could be given as homework and students could observe a coffee shop, skate park, or the mall on the weekend. The type of observation the students will be doing is nonparticipant observation; in other words, the students will not participate in the activities they are observing. Lesson 6 takes students through the steps of collecting observational data.

Practicing Data Analysis

The purpose of observing a cultural group from an ethnographic perspective is to discover the different *themes* and patterns that underlie the structure and function of a cultural group. One of the authors of this book completed an ethnography of an elementary school classroom as her dissertation research. In observing one third-grade classroom, Walker (2000) identified behavioral patterns that were repeated day after day in the classroom in lieu of a list of posted behavioral expectations or rules. These became the routines of the classroom. For example, the school day was arranged into different activities that called for different types of behaviors. These different activity times included Circle, Work, Story and Relax, Journals, and Silent Reading. During Circle time, the behavior expected of the students was to quietly listen to each other and raise their hands to speak, in contrast to Journals time, which was completed in total silence. As the author further analyzed the patterns, themes emerged that showed that these patterns of behavior were part of the routines that helped the classroom function efficiently. Lesson 7 takes students through the steps of data analysis.

Conclusion

Now is an opportune time to introduce the final project, a mini-ethnography, to the students. Each student will complete a mini-ethnography of a subcultural group he is interested in learning more about through the ethnography research process. The following list includes some ideas for students to start thinking about for a study of their subculture:

+ sports group (e.g., baseball, soccer, karate, track teams),
+ skate park,
+ church youth group,
+ debate team,
+ drama club,
+ chess club, or
+ cultural class/school (e.g., Chinese school).

Students will be thinking about a topic they might want to investigate as the class moves into Chapter 2, a study of culture.

Lesson 1: Assessing Students' Initial Knowledge

Objective: Students will complete a KWL to assess their knowledge of ethnography at the beginning of the unit.

Materials:
- ❍ KWL About Ethnography sheet, p. 20
- ❍ Pencils

Steps:
1. Ask students what kinds of things are discovered by research. Have a discussion of how research has impacted our society. The research the students do in this unit involves the social sciences. Research in the social sciences, or research about people, uses different methodology than research about inanimate objects. The students are probably more acquainted with scientific research than they are with social science research. Research in the social sciences, however, has a large impact on our society today. Opinion polls, focus groups, and surveys are often used to gauge people's perceptions, beliefs, and attitudes. Advertisers use this type of research frequently, as do politicians. As students use these research methods and see how they work, they will be able to become more critical evaluators of the research they see published.

2. Explain to students that the specific type of social science research they will be studying is ethnography. Ethnography is a type of study completed by anthropologists who study the origins of the physical, social, and cultural development of human beings. Ethnography is one way to study culture. An ethnographer is an anthropologist who becomes immersed in a culture to observe, record, and describe its culturally significant behaviors so others may better understand that culture (Fetterman, 1989). Ask students why this type of study might be important and create a list of their ideas and responses.

3. Tell students that in this unit of study, they will have the opportunity to become ethnographers and to study a culture of their interest. During the first part of the unit, students will be studying research methods and culture; in the final part, each student will conduct her own ethnographic study.

4. Give students the KWL chart found on page 20, and have them fill it out to gauge how much they know about research and ethnography.

5. Have students share their individual KWL charts to create a large KWL chart for the classroom. Have students add to both of these KWL charts as they complete this unit of study.

Evaluation: Students successfully complete a KWL chart.

Name: _____ Date: _____

KWL About Ethnography

Name: _____

What I Know	What I Want to Know	What I Learned

Exploring People and Cultures © Prufrock Press Inc.
Permission is granted to photocopy or reproduce this page for single classroom use only.

Lesson 2: Ethnographic Vocabulary

Objective: Students will be able to use the vocabulary words connected with ethnographic study.

Materials:
- ○ Ethnography Vocabulary list (see Appendix A), pp. 107–108
- ○ Wall space to create a classroom word wall
- ○ Ethnography Vocabulary Chart sheet, pp. 23–24

Steps:
1. Ask students what vocabulary words "science" brings to mind. On the board, create a list of words that pertain to the study of science.
2. Next, have students generate vocabulary words that apply to social science and ethnographic research. Write down any words they generate. Tell students they will be learning the vocabulary related to ethnography as they study this unit.
3. A list of words that pertain to ethnography can be found in Appendix A. You may introduce students to these words as they apply to the lesson or create a word wall of all of the words at the beginning of the unit.
4. An engaging way to have students study these new vocabulary words is to have them make up riddles for other students to solve using the words (Kingore, 2007) such as the ones below.
   a. I am a behavior. I am completed over and over. What am I? (Answer: Ritual)
   b. I am a belief. I am often formed unfairly. What am I? (Answer: Bias)

5. Additional vocabulary activities include:
   a. *Vocabulary Chart*: Use the Ethnography Vocabulary Chart (pp. 23–24) to gather ethnographic research words. Have students three-hole punch the form, and then place it in their research notebooks.
   b. *Wordle* (http://www.wordle.net): Wordle is a site for generating word clouds from words that the students provide. The clouds give greater prominence to words that appear more frequently in the source text. Students can tweak their word clouds with different fonts, layouts, and color schemes. Word clouds may be printed out or saved to the Wordle gallery to share with other students.

    c. *Trading Cards* (http://bighugelabs.com/flickr/deck.php): Students can create trading cards using their vocabulary words on this website. They may choose a picture that represents their word from the Internet, write a title and the word's definition, and then print out the cards or send them to each other by e-mail. Students can use these cards to learn the vocabulary words associated with this unit.

    d. *Flashcards* (http://www.iqfuse.com): The teacher may create online flashcards for the students on this site, and then students may visit the site to study the words.

Evaluation: By the end of the unit, students will be able to use the vocabulary words with understanding.

Name: _____   Date: _____

Ethnography Vocabulary Chart

Directions: Find words related to ethnography that begin with the letters of the alphabet. Give a definition for each word.

A	B
C	D
E	F
G	H
I	J
K	L
M	N

Exploring People and Cultures © Prufrock Press Inc.
Permission is granted to photocopy or reproduce this page for single classroom use only.

O	P
Q	R
S	T
U	V
W	X
Y	Z

Exploring People and Cultures © Prufrock Press Inc.

Permission is granted to photocopy or reproduce this page for single classroom use only.

Lesson 3: Populations and Samples

Note: This lesson was adapted from *About Teaching Mathematics: A K–8 Resource* (3rd ed.), by M. Burns, 2007, Sausalito, CA: Math Solutions Publications. Copyright 2007 by Math Solutions Publications. Adapted with permission.

Objective: Students will be able to make generalizations about a population from a sample.

Materials:
- ○ Small paper bag
- ○ Color tiles in two colors

Steps:
1. Place 10 tiles of two different colors (20 titles total) in a bag. Tell the students what you have done (without telling them how many of each color are in the bag). Go around the class, asking individual students to draw a tile out of the bag without looking, to note its color, and then return it to the bag.
2. Have a student record the colors that were drawn on the board. Do this for 10 draws and then have groups look at the information and decide whether or not they are willing to predict what is in the bag. Have groups share their opinions.
3. Then do 10 more draws, and again have groups discuss and share. Repeat this process as many times as needed for students to be able to predict or create a hypothesis about what is in the bag based on what they have learned from the previous draws.
4. At the end of the activity, take out the tiles and count how many tiles of each color are in the bag.
5. Have students discuss the accuracy of their hypotheses.
6. Explain to the students that what they have done is take a random sample of tiles to predict what the population of tiles is in the entire bag. At the end of this activity, have students reflect on how this type of research could be used with people.

Evaluation: Students are able to provide an explanation for generating their particular hypothesis and generalization.

Lesson 4: Surveys

Objective: Students will be able to design, complete, and analyze data from a survey.

Materials:
- ○ Paper
- ○ Fellow students or others to survey
- ○ Graph paper

Steps:
1. Have students gather in groups of four. These groups will design and administer a survey. Students may create a survey online using http://www.surveymonkey.com. First, the groups need to select a population such as the fifth grade. Next, the students need to decide what they want to find out. Do they want to know the sample students' favorite pets? What books they like to read? Their favorite sports? This question is called the research question.
2. Once they have their research question, students need to design a survey for others to complete. One popular type of survey is a Likert scale. A Likert scale provides a format asking respondents *to strongly agree, agree, disagree,* or *strongly disagree with* (or *to not approve, approve,* or *strongly approve of*) an issue or idea (Babbie, 1990). It is one way for students to design surveys. For example, students could ask other students their opinions of different school subjects using a Likert scale format, as shown in Figure 3.

Favorite Subjects of Students

1. I really enjoy math.
   Strongly agree   Agree   Disagree   Strongly disagree

2. My favorite subject is language arts.
   Strongly agree   Agree   Disagree   Strongly disagree

Figure 3. Sample Likert scale.

Another way to create a survey is to record the number of students who prefer different choices. For example, students ask others about their favorite type of pet and record the results in a chart similar to that in Figure 4. Student groups will create a survey with at least 10 questions.

Type of Pet	Number of People
Dog	
Cat	
Bird	
Fish	

Figure 4. Pet inventory chart.

3. Next, students decide how large a sample they will use. The number of people they survey will depend on the amount of time you have to devote to this activity and the availability of other classmates. The more people surveyed, the more generalizable the data are to the selected population.

4. After students collect their data, they need to analyze them. Analyzing survey data starts with adding up the number of responses for each question. Then students develop a table displaying their data, such as the one in Figure 5.

Type of Pet	Number of People
Dog	28
Cat	15
Bird	10
Fish	7

Figure 5. Pet survey example.

5. Have students transfer their data to a graph to help them to analyze their data. Students may decide what type of graph they will use. Figure 6 is an example of a graph. Students may create graphs on the computer using KidsGraph (http://nces.ed.gov/nceskids/createAgraph/default.aspx).

6. After analyzing their data, have students discuss with each other what they think their data mean. What attitude or behavior did they discover? In the example above, 47% of those surveyed chose dogs as their favorite animal. The data from this survey display that dogs are the respondents' favorite type of animal. If we generalize the results of these data to a larger population, dogs are the favorite type of pet of fifth-grade students.

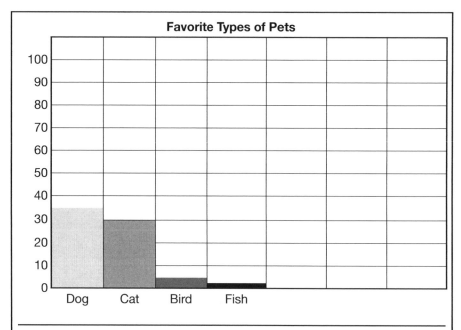

Favorite Types of Pets

Figure 6. Blank table for students to use to create a graph of their survey results.

Evaluation: Students are able to gather and analyze survey data and make a generalization from the results.

Lesson 5: Interviews

Objective: Students will be able to design, complete, and analyze data from an interview using an interview protocol.

Materials:
- Paper
- Access to people to interview
- Tape recorders or other taping devices

Steps:
1. In this activity, students will take the information they obtained in their surveys and develop questions to ask at least three respondents for additional information. Students will look at the data they obtained in the survey activity before creating their questions.
2. Students will design four to five interview questions. In the example from the previous lessons, students might ask the following questions of their interviewees:
   a. Why is a dog your favorite type of animal?
   b. What type of dog do you have?
   c. Have you ever had one of the other pets on the list?
   d. Would you ever consider getting one of the other types of animals? Why or why not?

3. Students then need to make arrangements to meet with several (at least three) individuals who participated in their initial surveys to ask these questions. Answers to the questions need to be recorded exactly as the respondent states them. Tape recorders, iPads, iPods, or some other type of recording device *must* be used to record answers. Because a recording device is used, the researcher may concentrate on the interviewee and will not be distracted by recording word-for-word answers by hand. Researchers will transcribe their data at a later time. Review the interview techniques listed by Koechlin and Zwaan (2006) and reprinted in Figure 7.

Questioning Etiquette and Guidelines

Good questioners get good results by following some basic guidelines, by being aware of the thoughts and ideas of others, and by just using good manners. To become an effective questioner:
- Listen to the thoughts and ideas of others.
- Don't interrupt others.
- Be mindful of the feelings and the privacy of others.
- Be aware of your own feelings.
- Respect others.
- Show appreciation.
- Stay on topic.

Figure 7. Questioning etiquette and guidelines. From *Q Tasks: The Student as Questioner*, by C. Koechlin and S. Zwaan, p. 110, 2006, Ontario, Canada: Pembroke Publishers. Copyright 2006 by Pembroke Publishers. Reprinted with permission.

4. Data analysis is different for interviews than surveys. Researchers look for similar answers to questions and put them into categories (called coding). Different-colored highlighters may be used to highlight similar answers after taped interviews have been transcribed. After the answers are highlighted, a table can be made that displays similar answers (see Figure 8). From these categories, researchers look for patterns in the answers of the interviewees.

    Looking at the table in Figure 8, the strongest pattern in the data is that dogs are friendly and fun to play with. Although it can't be generalized to a population that dogs are a favorite pet because they are friendly and fun to play with, the interviews may provide additional information about why survey participants made their particular choices.

    Please note to students that the more data they collect, the more they know about the sample of, and therefore the population of, the people they are researching. Researchers want to find out as much information as possible before they generate any conclusions.

Question	Interview 1	Interview 2	Interview 3	Interview 4
Why is a dog your favorite type of animal?	Friendly Loyal	Friendly Fun to play with	Friendly Fun to play with	Fun to play with Don't know
What type of dog do you have?	Westie	Golden Retriever	Portuguese Water Dog	Golden Retriever
Have you ever had any other pet on the list?	No	Yes, a fish	Yes, a bird	No
Would you ever consider getting another type of animal?	No	No, fish died	Yes	No

Figure 8. Sample pet interview patterns.

5. Have students share their interview data. Discussion the following: Did the data help students to find out more about the sample of people they studied with the interview after conducting the survey?

Evaluation: Students successfully design interview questions, complete interviews, and analyze data.

Lesson 6: Observational Data

Objective: Students will be able to take field notes and summarize them using sensory details and images.

Materials:
- ○ Access to a cultural group
- ○ Paper and pencils
- ○ Note cards or note pad
- ○ Tape recorders
- ○ Colored highlighters

Steps:
1. Tell students that they are now going to make observations of a cultural group. They will take field notes that will help them be able to describe this group. Culture, in this type of research, is any group of people who interact regularly and develop their own rituals, routines, values, and symbols. A classroom is a culture—as a school year evolves, classrooms become small societies with systems of rules, rituals, and traditions (Jackson, Boostrom, & Hansen, 1993). Write the following list on the board and have students think about these categories in relation to your classroom:
    a. exterior physical signs (e.g., shoes, clothing, jewelry, hair styles)
    b. expressive movement (e.g., body language, eye movement, facial expressions)
    c. physical location (e.g., setting, clustering, social distance, personal space)
    d. language behavior (e.g., conversations, amount of conversation)
    e. artifacts (objects made by people in the culture)
    f. symbols (artifacts that represent beliefs or customs of a cultural group)
    g. rituals (a repeated pattern of behavior that plays a part in cultural and social life)

    Have students describe your classroom culture based on these different areas. Try to get students to provide evidence for each of the seven areas of data. This will supply a concrete example of each type of data for the students.
2. Next, divide students into seven groups, one for each category listed. Each group will practice taking field notes on an assigned

category in the field. *Note*: This is an opportunity for the teacher to differentiate group membership based on ability, interest, or learning style.

3. Take students to a place to write field notes. In taking field notes, "the aim is to convey both the feeling as well as the facts of the observed event" (Fetterman, 1989, p. 114). Students observe and write field notes for the category they were given. *Writing Ethnographic Field Notes* (Emerson, Fretz, & Shaw, 1995) described the field note taking and observation process as consisting of the following:

> In attending to ongoing scenes, events, and interactions field researchers take mental notes of certain details and impressions. For the most part these impressions remain "headnotes" only. The field researcher makes brief written records of these impressions by jotting down key words and phrases. A word or two written at the moment or soon afterwards will jog the memory later in the day and enable the fieldworker to catch significant actions and to construct evocative descriptions of the scenes. (pp. 19–20)

Students will need to be careful to record the data accurately—they should not take any preconceived notions into the field. This may result in biased data. It might be useful to have a discussion about bias before students go into the field. After giving the students the definition of bias, ask them if they have ever heard anyone make a statement that might be considered biased. Have a discussion about how this bias might impact conclusions people make about each other. Discussion the following: If individuals use biased data, how will that affect their research?

4. When the students return to class, have them transcribe their field notes. The transcription of field notes will take a block of concentrated time. Students need to be as descriptive as possible. This description will present the reader with a picture of the scene and people through concrete sensory details and sensory imagery. Students can then use a three-hole punch and add the field notes to their research notebooks.

5. Have students get together with their other group members to discuss their field notes. Are their descriptions similar or different? Students will develop a group summary of their field notes to share with other category groups in the next lesson. To

integrate technology into this lesson, students could create an interactive poster summary online at http://edu.glogster.com. Remind students that it is important that they include sensory details and sensory imagery. They want to "paint a picture" in the readers' minds of the place and the people they observed.

Evaluation: Student groups write a summary that includes sensory images and details from their field notes.

Lesson 7: Data Analysis

Objective: Students will be able to generate patterns and themes from their data summaries.

Materials:
- ○ Student data (transcribed)
- ○ Paper to record themes and patterns

Steps:
1. Show the students the chart in Figure 9, which displays the patterns observed by Walker in one third-grade classroom.

Routines of the Classroom	
Activity Time	**Behavior**
Circle	One person speaks at a time; raise your hand to talk
Work	Talk quietly to the person next to you
Read and Relax	Quiet; no talking
Journals/Silent Reading	Quiet; no talking
Writing Workshop	Talk quietly; you may invite a friend to edit with you or listen to your writing

Figure 9. Patterns observed in one classroom.

2. Have students brainstorm some of the patterns of behavior that occur in your classroom. After recording them on the board, have students generate ideas on a theme that might explain these patterns. Are the patterns a part of the rituals and routines of the classroom, for example? Explain that these are the kinds of patterns and themes of behavior they will be looking for in the data they collected and transcribed.
3. Next, have students get together in groups that correspond to the different categories they were assigned to take field notes. Groups will have one person from each observational category. Have students share their summaries in their seven groups. Then, have students identify and record any patterns from their group's collective data.

4. Have each group choose a spokesperson to report to the larger group. The teacher will keep track of the reported patterns on the board for students.

5. After each group has shared, have the class investigate the list on the board for themes. A theme is a recurring, unifying subject or idea. The ethnographer begins with a mass of different ideas and behavior. As she analyzes the data, recurring events or patterns begin to emerge. After further analysis, themes emerge that explain the patterns (Fetterman, 1989). The patterns are the evidence that supports the theme.

6. Have the students generate one or two themes that might explain the patterns they found in their data.

7. Finally, as a class, discuss or have students blog about what was discovered about writing and analyzing field notes in this activity. What questions do they have about doing this process on their own?

Evaluation: Students proficiently generate patterns and themes from their summaries of data.

Chapter 2

A Student Ethnographer's Understanding of the Elements of Culture

Culture is complex, but it is not chaotic; there are clearly defined patterns to be discovered.

—Hofstede, Pederson, & Hofstede (2002, p. 87)

Culture is rather like the color of your eyes; you cannot change it or hide it, and although you cannot see it yourself, it is always visible to other people when you interact with them.

—Hofstede, Pederson, & Hofstede (2002, p. 196)

A second step in learning about ethnography is to understand culture. So what are cultures? Cultures are patterns of human behavior that include the beliefs, customs, artifacts, and institutions of any group of people. Cultures may be thought of in terms of distinct patterns and practices of behavior driven by the values and beliefs of members (Petracca & Sorapure, 2007). Students are members of many subcultural groups: families, schools, churches, neighborhoods, and sports teams, for example. Subcultural groups are groups within a culture. For example, a church community may have a teen group. The teen group could be considered a subculture within the larger church community group. Within student subcultural groups, like a teen church group or school choir, there are norms, values, and patterns that are spoken and unspoken. For example, in a chorus, are sopranos valued over altos? Is it better to be a short or tall student in the choir? Are soloists given more credence and respect from the music teacher or choir director and fellow choir members? How is a school choir member valued by the rest of the school community, including the administrators, teachers, paraprofessionals, other students, and parents?

To begin to identify and recognize some of the subcultural groups of students, complete Lesson 8. This exercise may open students up to an array of subcultural groups. The possibilities are endless.

After identifying, sharing, and discussing the student subcultures, have students keep the numerous examples in mind as they begin to explore a possible public research site for their own mini-ethnography. The student charts may be included in their research notebooks (Chapter 1), or they may be posted together on a classroom wall or bulletin board or on a class blog or wiki. Have students begin to think about a subculture that they would like to focus on as a possible venue for their upcoming study.

The Elements of Culture

All human beings belong to a culture and many subcultures. The norms, attitudes, stories, and artifacts of a culture are learned behaviors by members of any particular culture. Culture is important for many reasons, including order and a sense of community and belonging. An understanding of the elements of culture is critical to ethnographers. The universal elements of cultures include (Brown, 1995):

+ artifacts;
+ stories, histories, myths, legends, and jokes;
+ rituals, rites, ceremonies, and celebrations;
+ heroes;
+ symbols and symbolic action;
+ beliefs and assumptions;
+ attitudes; and
+ rules, norms, ethical codes, and values.

Lesson 9 will help students to identify the eight elements of culture listed by Brown (1995), while Lesson 10 will help students personalize their understanding of their family culture and apply their knowledge to the elements of culture.

For more experience with identifying the web of a common culture—family—complete the activity in Lesson 11 as a class to explore family behavior concerning affection. An alternative theme to showing affection might be how a family views and values an everyday task like having dinner. Lesson 11 will aid students as they turn toward an analysis of their own family's way of demonstrating affection. The final element of culture that students will focus on is cultural symbols, found in Lesson 12.

Once students are aware of culture and the eight elements of culture, it is time to move out into the field and to practice observing in one setting. Lesson 13 may aid students in identifying a specific culture in their world to explore for their mini-ethnography that will begin with Chapter 3's activities. Students will have many ideas after completing the activities in Lesson 8. Other students' ideas may help them to identify a cultural exploration site that excites them.

Conclusion

Adolescents involved in ethnographic research may develop a keen eye with insight into the elements of the subcultures they engage in presently and will engage in someday. Each student will be more successful as an individual and as a group member in the present and future when equipped with the skills of an ethnographer. In the next chapter, once students are familiar with the eight elements of culture and bias, they will roll up their sleeves and experience ethnographic research firsthand.

Lesson 8: Exploring Personal Subcultures

Objective: Students will identify five or more subcultural groups in which they participate.

Materials:
- ○ Student Subcultural Groups and Activities Chart, p. 41

Steps:
1. Lead students through a brief, whole-group discussion about examples of student subcultural groups.
2. Have students complete the Student Subcultural Groups and Activities Chart in order to apply and personalize their thinking about cultures and subcultures.
3. Have students compare and contrast their completed charts for a variety of examples with the person to their right by creating a simple Venn diagram. Teachers may visit the following websites for free and easily accessible copies of Venn diagrams and graphic organizers:
    a. http://www.eduplace.com/graphicorganizer/pdf/venn.pdf
    b. http://www.freeology.com

4. Students will share five discoveries with their group or class in a whole-group discussion.

Evaluation: Students will be able to demonstrate an understanding of their subcultural groups by completing the Student Subcultural Groups and Activities Chart.

Student Subcultural Groups and Activities Chart

Identify a subculture group or community where you spend time and/or effort.	Indicate the approximate amount of time spent with this group.
Example: Green Valley Middle School	5 days a week
Example: Shakespeare practice	2 times a week for 1 hour for one semester

Exploring People and Cultures © Prufrock Press Inc.
Permission is granted to photocopy or reproduce this page for single classroom use only.

Lesson 9: Identifying the Elements of Culture

Objective: Students will be able to identify the eight elements of culture by viewing and examining a film about a particular culture.

Material:
- Films
  - *Because of Winn Dixie (2005)*
  - *Holes (2003)*
  - *October Sky (1999)*
  - *The Secret of Roan Inish (2000)*
  - *Whale Rider (2003)*

  Note: The suggested movies are all PG (Parental Guidance); therefore, teachers *must* notify parent/s about the movie rating before viewing to obtain parental permission.
- Step In/Step About/Step Out sheet, p. 44
- Jigsaw the Eight Elements of Culture sheet, p. 45

Steps:
1. View two 30-minute segments of one of the films (*Whale Rider* is one of the best cultural film examples) for practice experiencing, observing, and identifying the eight elements of culture.
2. Before viewing the two film clips, give each student a copy of the Step In/Step About/Step Out activity. Have students view the film with their senses in mind. Students will record the observations they make about the culture viewed.
3. After viewing the two 30-minute segments of the selected film and completing the Step In/Step About/Step Out activity, students will then jigsaw the eight elements of culture (see Appendix B for an explanation of jigsaw and other differentiation methods). Give each student a copy of the Jigsaw the Eight Elements of Culture sheet (p. 45). Each student will volunteer or will be assigned to complete at least one of the eight pieces of the culture jigsaw. On a large sheet of butcher-block paper, paste together the eight pieces of culture completed by the students for the observed film.

Evaluation: Students will understand the eight elements of culture through the discussion of the film and the completion of the two activities.

If repetition is needed for the core concept of understanding the elements of culture that are central to ethnographic research, then the

Step In/Step About/Step Out and Jigsaw activities may be repeated using a book such as:

- *Bridge to Teribithia* by Katherine Paterson (1977)
- *Because of Winn Dixie* by Kate DiCamillo (2000)
- *Holes* by Louis Sachar (1998)
- *Of Beetles and Angels: A Boy's Remarkable Journey From a Refugee Camp to Harvard* by Mawi Asgedom (2002)
- *To Kill a Mockingbird* by Harper Lee (1960)
- *Where the Red Fern Grows* by Wilson Rawls (1961)

The book selection will depend on the age level, reading ability, and interest of the group of students undertaking the study of ethnographic research.

Name: _____ Date:_____

Step In/Step About/Step Out

Using your senses, complete the following chart as you are viewing the selected movie clips.

What do you see?	What do you hear?	What do you smell?

Note. From *Q Tasks: The Student as Questioner*, by C. Koechlin and S. Zwann, 2006, Ontario, Canada: Pembroke Publishers. Copyright 2006 by Pembroke Publishers. Adapted with permission.

Exploring People and Cultures © Prufrock Press Inc.
Permission is granted to photocopy or reproduce this page for single classroom use only.

Jigsaw the Eight Elements of Culture

Each student will volunteer to complete one of the eight pieces by recording the selected element of culture after watching the selected movie.

Artifacts	**Stories, Histories, Myths, Legends, and Jokes**
Rituals, Rites, Ceremonies, and Celebrations	**Heroes**
Symbols and Symbolic Action	**Beliefs and Assumptions**
Attitudes	**Rules, Norms, Ethical Codes, and Values**

Exploring People and Cultures © Prufrock Press Inc.
Permission is granted to photocopy or reproduce this page for single classroom use only.

Lesson 10: Synthesizing Personal Cultures

Objective: Students will research their family's cultural background and will share one of the preselected elements of culture with a small group and the rest of the class.

Materials:
- ○ Your Cultural Heritage letter to parent(s), p. 47
- ○ Personal Culture Checklist, p. 48
- ○ Products List, p. 49

Steps:
1. Read the Your Cultural Heritage letter to parents as a class. Send the letter home to each student's parent(s)/guardian(s). Explain this activity thoroughly to students.
2. Set dates and deadlines with students on the Personal Culture Checklist.
3. Break the students up into eight groups. Give each of the eight groups one of the elements of culture on an index card.
4. Set a timeline for students to gather family cultural information to bring back to their small group. In class, give students time to share their gathered information, especially about their selected element of culture.
5. Give students a copy of the Products List on page 49. Have them be creative in the way they share their group's cultural results. They may use one of the activities on the Products List, or they may negotiate with the teacher to create a product not listed.
6. Each student will contribute in some way to the product they are producing. Have each of the eight groups share its product.

Evaluation: Students will demonstrate their learning of one cultural element by the creation, completion, and sharing of a summary of family cultural findings in one of eight small groups.

Your Cultural Heritage

Dear Parent(s)/Guardian(s),

As part of the study of ethnographic research, your child will be learning about the eight elements of culture. Each child will research with you at home to find out as much as possible about your family's ancestors. You may have multiple countries in your heritage. It may be helpful to focus on one of your family's ancestors.

Each student will be sharing his or her cultural heritage with a small group at school and reporting about one of the eight elements of culture (stories, heroes, symbols, beliefs/assumptions, attitudes, values, rituals/ceremonies, and artifacts). Then students will report the results of their group with a product of their choice to the entire class. Some of the questions that they may ask you that will be helpful are:

1. *Stories:* What are some of the stories from your ancestors? Where did they come from?
2. *Heroes:* Did they endure any hardships? Are there stories about any heroes or heroines in our family?
3. *Symbols:* What clothes, gestures, or other symbols did our ancestors pass down to us?
4. *Beliefs/Assumptions:* What are some common beliefs that our ancestors had?
5. *Attitudes:* Are there attitudes still prevalent that we inherited from our ancestors?
6. *Values:* What did our ancestors value that we still value today?
7. *Rituals/Ceremonies:* What customs or beliefs do we still practice that have been handed down from our ancestors?
8. *Artifacts:* Are there any physical things (e.g., photos, books, maps, symbols, material objects) that are indicative of our cultural heritage?

You may want to join us for the group sharing of this activity. We will let you know the product-sharing schedule. If you send any artifacts, we promise to take great care of them and return them safely home. Or, you may bring them to the sharing session, if you so desire.

We intend to be respectful of each family's customs, beliefs, and culture. It is our hope that this exercise will help to foster a better understanding and appreciation of each family's heritage. These exercises will also promote an understanding and practical application of the eight elements of culture.

Do not hesitate to call or e-mail with your questions.

Please sign and return this letter or a copy of the letter to your child's teacher.

Teacher's signature: _____

Phone and/or e-mail address:_____

Parent's signature: _____

Exploring People and Cultures © Prufrock Press Inc.
Permission is granted to photocopy or reproduce this page for single classroom use only.

Name: _____ Date:_____

Personal Culture Checklist

Activity	Student Plan	Date Due
1. Your Cultural Heritage letter to parent(s)/guardian(s) signed.	Parents send electronically signed copy or hard copy to teacher.	
2. Students organize into eight groups and receive one index card with one element of culture.	Students organize into eight small groups either sorted by the teacher or by student choice.	
3. Students gather family cultural information.	Students share gathered information with other students, with particular attention given to the group's assigned element of culture.	
4. In small groups, students utilize the Products List to select a way to present their family cultural information.	Students use the Products List to creatively plan and present a summary of their element of culture.	
5. Students present their final product for their element of culture.	In their small group, each student will present part of the final presentation of his or her element of culture.	
6. Build a classroom display of the eight elements of culture.	Each small group will display its element of culture, if possible.	

Exploring People and Cultures © Prufrock Press Inc.

Permission is granted to photocopy or reproduce this page for single classroom use only.

Products List

Diary entry	Interview on a taped radio show	Diorama
Pamphlet	Rubbing	Timeline
Period costume	Dramatic monologue	Map
Play/skit	Dance	Memoir
Song	Sonnet	Poem
Puppet show	Vodcast	Podcast
PowerPoint presentation	Animoto presentation	Prezi presentation
Family stories on VoiceThread.com	Garage band production	Student suggestion

Exploring People and Cultures © Prufrock Press Inc.
Permission is granted to photocopy or reproduce this page for single classroom use only.

Lesson 11: Beliefs and Assumptions: Family Affection

Objective: Students will learn that different family cultures demonstrate affection in different ways (e.g., embraces, kisses, slight punches on the arm, handshakes, no physical contact, loving glances).

Materials:
- Paper
- Pencil
- Posterboard or access to a computer for two groups
- Tape recorder for one group
- Family Affection Tasks for Group 1 sheet, p. 51
- Family Affection Tasks for Group 2 sheet, p. 52
- Family Affection Tasks for Group 3 sheet, p. 53

Steps:
1. Students will be sorted into three groups to discuss how their families demonstrate affection. Then, each group will be assigned an activity to share with the entire class. Prior to this activity, the teacher may assign students deliberately into three tiered groups. The teacher will record the three group assignments on three index cards with the names of the students in each of the three groups.
   a. Group 1: Each student in Group 1 will be given the Family Affection Tasks for Group 1 sheet on page 51. Each student will tell how his or her family demonstrates affection. Summarize the group's discussion in a drawing or diagram that includes the contributions of all group members.
   b. Group 2: Each student in Group 2 will be given the Family Affection Tasks for Group 2 sheet on page 52. Each group member will share how his or her family demonstrates affection. Students will classify the results on a student-generated chart to be shared with the whole class.
   c. Group 3: Each student in Group 3 will be given the Family Affection Tasks for Group 3 sheet on page 53. Each student will tell how his or her family demonstrates affection. The group will create a song that includes all responses and will share the song with the whole class.

2. All groups will share their products during a wrap-up at the end of the class.

Evaluation: Each group will demonstrate how families show affection by producing and sharing a group-created final product.

Family Affection Tasks for Group 1

Day 1	Students will have observed their family members and had a family discussion in order to bring back examples to their group about how they show affection.
Day 2	Students will share their observations and examples with other group members. Students will begin to plan a way to illustrate through a diagram or drawing a group summary of the ways that their families share affection. Students will begin the diagram or drawing.
Day 3	Students will complete their diagram or drawing. They will share it with the whole class.

Exploring People and Cultures © Prufrock Press Inc.
Permission is granted to photocopy or reproduce this page for single classroom use only.

Family Affection Tasks for Group 2

Day 1	Students will have observed their family members and had a family discussion in order to bring back examples to their group about how they show affection.
Day 2	Students will share their observations and examples with other group members. Students will begin to plan a way to classify and categorize all student observations and responses in a chart.
Day 3	Students will complete their chart. They will share their chart with the whole group.

Exploring People and Cultures © Prufrock Press Inc.
Permission is granted to photocopy or reproduce this page for single classroom use only.

Family Affection Tasks for Group 3

Day 1	Students will have observed their family members and had a family discussion in order to bring back examples to their group about how they show affection.
Day 2	Students will share their observations and examples with other group members. Students will begin to plan a way to classify and categorize all student observations and responses. Students will begin to create and write a song about their collective observations and experiences.
Day 3	Students will complete the writing of their song. They will practice singing their song together. When they are ready, they will sing their song about family affection together.

Exploring People and Cultures © Prufrock Press Inc.
Permission is granted to photocopy or reproduce this page for single classroom use only.

Lesson 12: Symbols

Objective: Students will identify symbols from their culture or one of their subcultures identified in the first lesson in this chapter.

Materials:
- Student Subcultural Groups and Activities Chart sheet (p. 41), completed
- Computer to design a PowerPoint or other technological application agreed upon with the teacher

Steps:
1. Students will choose one of their subcultures from their completed Student Subcultural Groups and Activities Chart.
2. Students will download their own photos or cut and paste pictures to create a PowerPoint, Prezi, or online poster (http://Glogster.com/edu) with at least five symbols of one of their subcultures.

Evaluation: All students will demonstrate their knowledge of their family's symbols or one of their identified subcultures by completing a technological product (e.g., Powerpoint, Prezi, online poster) that will be shared with the entire class.

Lesson 13: Describing Personal Culture, Subculture, Biases, and Attitudes

Objective: Students will complete a one-hour field observation of a subculture from their completed Student Subcultural Groups and Activities Chart from the first lesson in this chapter or from an idea shared by another classmate. Students will examine their reactions to their field observation and their personal biases.

Material:
- Field notebook
- Site for observations
- Adult supervision
- List of questions, below
- Field Observation Essay Rubric, p. 57

Steps:
1. Each student will receive a Field Observation Essay Rubric on page 57. Prior to and after going out into the field and observing, the students will complete some careful thinking about what they know and what they think they know about themselves and their selected subcultural site. Student researcher questions to ponder and to incorporate into their first field observation experience include:
   a. Why did you choose this site?
   b. Are you a participant or a nonparticipant of this subculture?
   c. State the preconceived notions that you may have about this site before observing it.
   d. What is your background (e.g., age, race, gender, socioeconomic status)?
   e. How does your background have an impact on your perceptions of what you are observing in the field?
   f. Discuss surprises or insights you have after completing your field observation.

2. Students will immerse themselves for at least one hour as a participant or nonparticipant at their selected site. Students will write a 1–2-page essay reporting their observations, reactions, and biases immediately following their visit to the site.
3. Hard copies of the field observation essay will be saved in the research notebook. Essays will also be posted on the class blog set up by the teacher.

Evaluation: Students will experience a field observation of one of their selected subcultures and record notes about the elements of culture and their experienced biases. The first field observation exercise may help students to identify the ethnographic site they will study for their mini-ethnographic study to be completed in forthcoming chapters.

Technology Challenge: Interested students may write, produce, film, and/or publish a videocast (vodcast), podcast, or other application of a Web 2.0 tool explaining bias as they may have experienced it in Lesson 13 during the field observation experience or during any of the other lessons in this chapter.

Field Observation Essay Rubric

Category	4	3	2	1
Field observation	For one hour or more	For 45 minutes or less	For 30 minutes or less	Did not complete the field observation
Explanation of subculture site chosen	Clearly and concisely written with reason for the subculture choice	Explanation stated	Explanation not totally clear	Subculture site chosen, but not observed
Participant explanation	Clearly and concisely written with simple statements about participant or nonparticipant status	Explanation stated	Explanation not totally clear	Participant explanation made from memory and not through field observation
Preconceived notions discussed	Clearly and concisely written with personal insights into preconceived stereotypes or prejudices	Explanation stated	Explanation not totally clear	Without field observation experience, preconceived notions cannot be noted
Personal background (e.g., age, race, gender, socioeconomic status) information impact	Clearly and concisely written with a self-awareness of student's own personal background	Explanation stated	Explanation not totally clear	Personal background information not impactful without field observation experience
Surprises or insights	Clearly and concisely written	Explanation stated	Explanation not totally clear	Insights not possible without field observation experience

Exploring People and Cultures © Prufrock Press Inc.
Permission is granted to photocopy or reproduce this page for single classroom use only.

Chapter 3

Student Mini-Ethnographic Proposal

> *Writing is hard work. Writing well is even harder. Ethnography requires good writing skills at every state of the enterprise.*
>
> —Fetterman (1989, p. 104)

Proposing a Mini-Ethnography

Now that the students have learned some basics of research and something about cultures, they will do some research and propose their mini-ethnography. Creating a proposal provides the opportunity to think about what subculture they want to study and how they will go about completing their project. Learning to write a proposal is a valuable skill that students may use as they continue on through high school and college. It is one form of persuasive writing.

Students will first brainstorm some ideas about what they want to study by using the activities in Lesson 14. Researchers survey the literature about their topic before they begin their research. The literature review in Lesson 15 may help to provide more information about the subculture under study. This exercise will help the students gauge whether enough information exists to proceed with their topic.

After the students have confirmed that their topic is viable, they will write a purpose statement for their project using the guidance in Lesson 16. After students have completed their Topic Browsing Planners and their purpose statements, they are ready to propose and begin their mini-ethnography using Lesson 17. Students will need to make some observations of their chosen group. Field research is the method that defines ethnography—the number of observations required will depend on time and students' access to appropriate groups. Observations and interviews can be given as homework assignments. Parents will need to support students in making observations and conducting interviews. If this is not possible, the teacher may opt to have these students do their research on a group that is available to them during school hours, such as another classroom. Another option is to have these students use technology and the library to complete their projects. The students could do research of a culture using the Internet and books available in the school library. The students could then set up interviews either on the phone or through e-mail and develop their ethnographies based on these data.

A Letter to Parents

At this time, a letter will be sent out to apprise parents of the study (see Figure 10 for a sample letter). Students will need to do some of the ethnography work outside of class, including observations. Parents will need to be a support system for the students in completing this project.

Some Thoughts on Writing

Writing the proposal will help students clarify their thinking. "In sitting down to put thoughts on paper, an individual must organize those thoughts and sort out the specific ideas and relationships" (Fetterman, 1989, p. 105) and explain them to others. One of the main goals of this unit is to have students learn to use research tools in context. By this time, students will have spent time doing research in the library, developing different types of research projects, and writing them up. These skills will be invaluable as the students continue their education. The writing that the students do now for their proposal will be clear and will display how their final papers will be organized. As the quote says in the beginning of this chapter, "Writing is hard work. Writing well is even harder" (Fetterman, 1989, p. 104). Students need to know that writing is hard, but they may learn to do it well with practice, and writing the proposal is excellent practice for the future. Figure 11 includes a rubric you may use for evaluating students' research proposals.

Date:_____

Dear Parent(s)/Guardian(s):

Our class is excited to begin an ethnographic study. Ethnography is a form of scientific study that focuses on human culture. Students will have the opportunity to become anthropologists and get immersed in a culture to observe, record, and describe it. Students will choose a culture to study. Part of this study will involve observing this culture in action. This is called fieldwork. Your child will require you to take him or her to observe others for 1 hour on three separate occasions. Students may also need to interview someone who is a representative of the culture they have chosen.

Students have already begun to learn that culture in ethnography is broader than an ethnic group. Culture is the rituals and routines that define different groups of people. Classrooms and offices have their own cultures, as do sports teams, skate parks, clubs, and other groups. Please encourage your child to research something that he or she is interested in, as this will make the project more enjoyable. The purpose of ethnography is not to look critically at a cultural group, but just to describe it to others. The objective of this type of research is to better understand our world and the people in it.

Students will need a three-ring binder to use as a research notebook. All papers related to the study will be placed in their notebooks, including rough drafts of the final paper. The organizational skills developed in completing a long-term project are important as your student moves through the rest of his or her schooling.

We will have a culminating activity where students will share their learning as the projects are completed. Completing this research project will be a challenging and rewarding activity for your child, and I appreciate your support.

Sincerely,

Figure 10. Sample letter to parents.

	4	**3**	**2**	**1**
Organization	Information is very organized with well-constructed paragraphs and subheadings.	Information is organized with well-constructed paragraphs.	Information is organized, but paragraphs are not well constructed.	Information is disorganized.
Purpose statement	Purpose statement clearly captures the essence of the study.	Purpose statement states the purpose of the study.	Purpose statement is not totally clear.	Purpose statement is unclear.
Data-gathering strategies	Data-gathering strategies are clearly delineated and explained.	Data-gathering strategies are listed and explained but are not totally clear.	Data-gathering strategies are listed but not explained.	Data-gathering strategies are not clearly listed or explained.
Final presentation	The creative presentation piece is extremely well explained and tied to the purpose of the study.	The creative presentation is explained and tied to the purpose of the study.	The creative presentation is explained, but not tied to the purpose of the study.	The creative presentation piece of the study is not well explained.
Mechanics	No grammatical, spelling, or punctuation errors.	Almost no grammatical, spelling, or punctuation errors.	A few grammatical, spelling, or punctuation errors.	Many grammatical, spelling, or punctuation errors.

Figure 11. Research proposal rubric.

Lesson 14: Brainstorming

Objective: Students will brainstorm ideas for their ethnographic project using a brainstorming web.

Materials:
- ○ Brainstorming Web sheet, p. 64
- ○ Pencils

Steps:
1. Remind students that throughout the study of research methods and culture, they might have been thinking about ideas for completing their own mini-ethnography. In this activity, students will complete a brainstorming web in which they will brainstorm ideas for their own projects.
2. Some questions for the students to consider as they brainstorm their ideas:
   a. What is your family's ethnic origin? Would learning more about this culture interest you?
   b. Is there a certain culture that interests you?
   c. Is there a particular place you're interested in finding out more about? Can you research the culture of that place?
   d. Are there cultural groups that have just immigrated to your area? Are there any that interest you?

3. Have students complete the Brainstorming Web on page 64.

Evaluation: Students successfully complete the Brainstorming Web.

Name: _____ Date:_____

Brainstorming Web

Name:

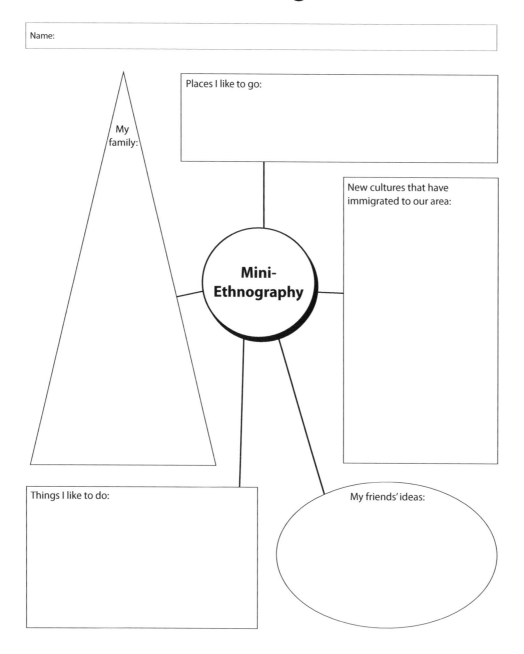

Places I like to go:

My family:

New cultures that have immigrated to our area:

Mini-Ethnography

Things I like to do:

My friends' ideas:

Exploring People and Cultures © Prufrock Press Inc.
Permission is granted to photocopy or reproduce this page for single classroom use only.

Lesson 15: Browsing Planner for Ethnographic Study

Objective: Students will summarize and organize information about a subculture from multiple sources by taking notes, outlining ideas, and completing a graphic organizer.

Materials:
- ○ Browsing Planner for Ethnographic Study sheet, p. 67
- ○ Access to the Internet and research materials
- ○ Pencils

Steps:
1. Take students to the library or computer lab to examine sources about their topic of interest. The questions driving this activity are:
   a. Is enough information about this culture or group available? Consider these sources:
      i. Internet
      ii. Public library
      iii. Museums

   b. What are some community resources that can be used? Consider these resources:
      i. Experts
      ii. Friends
      iii. Relatives

   c. Is it possible to do fieldwork?
   d. Will interviews be possible?
   e. Are videos or other media accessible and available?

2. Give students each a copy of the Browsing Planner for Ethnographic Study (Winebrenner, 1992) found on page 67. Explain to students that primary sources are original, firsthand accounts created at the time of the event. Secondary sources are secondhand accounts published or created after primary sources that often cite primary sources. Students may spend their time finding as much information as they can about their topic.
3. Students may take the browsing planner home for homework and ask their parents and friends about additional sources for their research.

Evaluation: Students will successfully complete the Browsing Planner for Ethnographic Study. If enough information cannot be located about a topic, the student should choose a different topic for study.

Name: _____ Date: _____

Browsing Planner for Ethnographic Study

Topic I am interested in studying: _____

Information Sources	Author, Name of Group or Individual	Title	Where I Found It
Primary Sources			
Secondary Sources			
Possible Fieldwork Sites			
Possible Interview Subjects			
Survey Ideas			

Note. Adapted from *Teaching Gifted Kids in the Regular Classroom: Strategies and Techniques Every Teacher Can Use to Meet the Academic Needs of the Gifted and Talented (Revised and Updated Edition)* by Susan Winebrenner, © 2001, 1992. Used with permission of Free Spirit Publishing Inc., Minneapolis, MN: 800-735-7323; www.freespirit.com. All rights reserved.

67

Permission is granted to photocopy or reproduce this page for single classroom use only.

Lesson 16: The Purpose Statement

Objective: Students will write a purpose statement that establishes the purpose for their mini-ethnographies.

Materials:
- ○ Writing a Strong Purpose Statement sheet, p. 69
- ○ Pencils

Steps:
1. Explain to students that the purpose statement provides the research question and establishes the purpose of their study. It will explain to others what the student is hoping to find out. All of the data the students gather will be related to the purpose statement.
2. Give students a copy of the handout that provides ideas for writing a purpose statement and the script.
3. In *Research Design: Qualitative and Quantitative Approaches*, Creswell (1994) provided some suggestions for writing a good purpose statement:
   a. Use words such as purpose, intent, or objective to call attention to this statement as the purpose of the study.
   b. Clearly mention the element of culture being explored or understood in the study.
   c. Include words that explain the method of inquiry to be used in data collection, analysis, and the process of research.
   d. Mention the research site (e.g., classroom, organization, program, event) for the study.
   e. Use scripting. Scripting is a process of completing blanks in a sentence, based on cues in the sentence. An example of a script that the students could use for their purpose statement is:
      The purpose of this study is to _____ (understand? describe? discover?) the _____ (element of culture) for _____ (culture or subculture) using an ethnographic design resulting in a _____ (cultural picture? description of themes and patterns?).

4. Have students use the Writing a Strong Purpose Statement on page 69 to practice writing their purpose statements. To include the use of technology, the teacher may post the purpose statement on the blog for students to complete and share with each other.

Evaluation: Students complete a well-written purpose statement that describes their proposed study.

Name: _____ Date: _____

Writing a Strong Purpose Statement

When writing a strong purpose statement,

1. Use words such as purpose, intent, or objective to call attention to this statement as the purpose idea in the study.

2. Clearly mention the element of culture being explored or understood in the study.

3. Include words that explain the method of inquiry to be used in data collection, analysis, and completion of research.

4. Mention the unit culture, subculture, or research site (e.g., classroom, organization, program, or event) for the study.

Practice writing a purpose statement using the following script:

The purpose of this study is to _____ (understand? describe? discover?) the _____ (element of culture) for _____ (culture or subculture) using an ethnographic design resulting in a _____ (cultural picture? description of themes and patterns?).

After completing and sharing this activity with your teacher, insert this page in your research notebook.

Exploring People and Cultures © Prufrock Press Inc.
Permission is granted to photocopy or reproduce this page for single classroom use only.

Lesson 17: Writing Your Research Proposal

Objective: Students will design a research project that includes a research question, ways of collecting and analyzing data using ethnographic methods of research, and a written and oral presentation of their findings.

Materials:
- Completed Browsing Planner for Ethnographic Study sheet (see Lesson 15, p. 67)
- Purpose statement handout
- Notes from library research
- Rubric for research proposal (see Figure 11, p. 62)
- Pencils/paper

Steps:
1. Explain to students that each research proposal will need to include:
   a. a purpose statement;
   b. the strategies for gathering data: observations, interviews, or surveys;
   c. other sources of data: books, Internet articles, or videos (called document analysis); and
   d. how the student will present his or her findings.

   The final project will include both a written research report and an oral presentation. The oral presentation element of the project is where the students may infuse their creativity into the project. Some products for the oral presentation to be discussed and planned in Chapter 5 include: animation, Animoto, audiotape, documentary, Glogster, magazine, movie, museum exhibit, newscast, oral history, photo journal, podcast, Power-Point presentation, video, and visual arts project.

2. Give each student a copy of the rubric for the research proposal (found on p. 62) and go over the expectations. Research shows that providing students with clear rubrics or criteria lists to writing assignments improves student achievement in writing (Overmeyer, 2009a).

Evaluation: Students successfully complete a research proposal with all necessary components outlined.

Chapter 4

Completing the
Mini-Ethnography

> *You never really understand a person until you consider things from his*
> *point of view—until you climb into his skin and walk around in it.*
> —Lee (1960, p. 39)

Ethnographic Research Applied

Students will now be engaged in completing their own mini-ethnographies and writing up the results. Observations and interviews may be completed as homework assignments, but there will be some class time to allow students to transcribe and analyze their data. During this chapter, take some time to read some sections of ethnographies to the students so they get an idea of what their final papers will be like. Suggestions are included in Appendix C.

The first lesson in the chapter, Lesson 18, provides the students with an opportunity to create a timeline for completing their ethnography, so they will be able to chunk the project into manageable parts. It also has them review the rubric for the project and create a checklist of what is required in the completed document. Both of these activities will help students become prepared for writing.

In Lesson 19, students will go to the library or media center to research background information for their topic. Students start creating notecards at this point, and it is important to make sure students understand this process and are organizing their notecards so they will be able to use them effectively in writing their reports.

Creating a map of the community (Overmeyer, 2009b) will help the ethnographer with his or her thinking. Like writing, mapmaking forces the ethnographer to use abstract thinking to reduce reality to a manageable size, a piece of paper (Fetterman, 1989). Lesson 20 will help students create a helpful visual representation of the community they are studying. This lesson will be taught after they have completed two field observations. In this activity, students create a map of their observation site. After the map is created, students can use it to generate topics for their writing assignment.

Lesson 21 will have the students pick an area on the map they created of their community and write a detailed description of it as practice in descriptive writing. As discussed in this book's introduction, the ethnographer tries to get a detailed understanding of the group she is studying and then describe this understanding to others so the readers will obtain a better understanding of cultural behavior and point of view.

After students have completed at least two observations, they will start sorting their data (Lesson 22) and identifying patterns. Fetterman (1989) stated that data analysis in ethnography has no single form or stage, and that analysis starts when the students first begin to gather data and continues throughout the data-gathering process. Time will be given every week for students to work with their data throughout the project. After students have found at least three patterns in their data, it is time for the next lesson, analyzing themes (Lesson 23).

Lesson 24 will have the students cluster their themes and patterns. Suggest that students limit their themes to three. Themes and patterns may not go together as neatly on the graphic organizer handout in Lesson 24 as students expect. Students might need to sort and resort their data a few times before they are clear about how the patterns and themes work together to identify behavior patterns of observed groups. Once students complete their graphic organizers, it is time to move on to Lesson 25, in which students create a thesis statement for their reports.

Synthesizing is an important step in the research cycle; it is a process similar to working a jigsaw puzzle (Harvey, 1998). In the same way people manipulate puzzle pieces to form a new picture, students will need to arrange their fieldwork notes in Lesson 25 to create new knowledge about a culture (McKenzie, 1996). Synthesizing takes summarizing to the next level; whereas summarizing is a brief retelling of what the researchers found, synthesizing involves the students' personal reaction to the research, what was learned, and why the students think their information adds to the knowledge about the culture or subculture (Harvey, 1998).

Lesson 26 has the students outline their papers. A particular type of outline is not required, but at this point, students need to start to chunk their information into individual subtopics so that they can write their research reports. After outlining, students will write their lead sentences (Lesson 27). Different forms of effective leads are discussed as a class, and students choose which one they think will be most effective in "hooking" their readers.

Verbatim quotes (word for word) are an important part of ethnographic reporting. They exemplify the people's thoughts and feelings. Quotes convey the emotions of the humans involved in a given situation (Fetterman, 1989). A researcher may have reams of wonderful data, but the spoken words of a person bring the writing alive like nothing else (Portalupi & Fletcher, 2001). Students will choose their quotes carefully to strengthen their writing and support what they are trying to convey to the reader in Lesson 28.

Harvey (1998) emphasized how crucial endings are. A good ending to an ethnography will capture the essence of the study, wrap things up, and end with a memorable final sentence that brings closure to the piece. Lesson 29 will help students strengthen their concluding paragraphs.

Editing is an essential step in the writing process, but one that is difficult for many students. Have students share their drafts of their research reports with each other during the writing process. Editing a little bit at a time is less overwhelming than editing an entire report. Lesson 30 will provide students with a checklist for the final edit after the paper is completed.

Once students have completed writing their final research reports, they will share and compare their mini-ethnographies, not that they haven't had the opportunity to view and experience each other's work throughout this course of study. In Chapter 5, students will share what they have learned to other interested parties: parents, family members, students, and other school community members. The suggested culminating activity, a demonstration fair, will be planned and implemented by the students. Final sharing and evaluating activities are included in the final chapter.

Lesson 18: Practical Preparation: Creating a Timeline and Checklist for the Ethnographic Study

Objective: Students will create a timeline and a checklist for the completion of their project.

Materials:
- ◯ Suggested Mini-Ethnography Project Timeline sheet, p. 75
- ◯ Browsing Planner for Ethnographic Study sheet (see Lesson 15, p. 67)
- ◯ Rubric for Final Mini-Ethnography Research Report, p. 76

Steps:
1. Students will use their Browsing Planner for Ethnographic Study to help them create a timeline for their mini-ethnography. As the teacher, you will need to decide how much in-class time will be devoted to this project and how much time will be spent outside of class.
2. A suggested timeline is included in the Suggested Mini-Ethnography Project Timeline sheet on page 75. Students are given a week to complete each step of the process. This timeline assumes that students are doing their observations and interviews as homework, but have one or two class periods a week to transcribe their data and write their reports in the classroom setting. A copy of the timeline should be sent home to parents as well.
3. Another step in the preparation process is for the class to review the rubric on page 76 and create a checklist with the items they will need to guide and complete their report at the proficient or advanced level. This class chart could be written on butcher-block paper and displayed in the classroom.

Evaluation: Students complete a timeline and checklist for the completion of their mini-ethnographies.

Name: _____ Date:_____

Suggested Mini-Ethnography Project Timeline

Week 1   Visit media center for research on subculture of
choice/set up observations   _____

Week 2   First observation/transcribe field notes   _____

Week 3   Second observation/transcribe field notes/sort data   _____

Week 4   Third observation/transcribe field notes/sort data   _____

Week 5   Interview 1 and/or survey   _____

Week 6   Interview 2 and/or survey   _____

Week 7   Analyze data and identify patterns   _____

Week 8   Identify themes from patterns   _____

Week 9   Writers' workshop   _____

Week 10   Writers' workshop continued/edit   _____

Week 11   Plan for demonstration fair   _____

Exploring People and Cultures © Prufrock Press Inc.
Permission is granted to photocopy or reproduce this page for single classroom use only.

Rubric for Final Mini-Ethnography Research Report

Category	4	3	2	1
Organization	Information is very organized with well-constructed paragraphs and subheadings.	Information is organized with well-constructed paragraphs and subheadings.	Information is organized, but paragraphs and subheadings are not well-constructed.	Information appears to be disorganized.
Thesis statement	The thesis statement very clearly states the purpose of the research.	The thesis statement states the purpose of the research	The thesis statement is not totally clear.	The thesis statement is unclear.
Presentation of information	The information is engagingly written using descriptive language. It paints a clear picture of the culture.	The information is well written and descriptive language is used to paint a picture of the culture.	Information is presented describing the culture, but a clear picture is not created.	The information presented does not describe the culture of the group under study.
Explanation of data-gathering strategies	Data-gathering strategies are very clear and concisely written.	Data-gathering strategies are listed and explained, but are not totally clear.	Data-gathering strategies are listed, but not explained.	Data-gathering strategies are not clearly listed or explained.
Evidence	Evidence clearly supports the themes and patterns described in the report.	Evidence provides some support for the themes and patterns described in the report.	Evidence provides little support for the themes and patterns described in the report.	Evidence does not support the themes and patterns described in the report.
Mechanics	No grammatical, spelling, or punctuation errors.	Almost no grammatical, spelling, or punctuation errors.	A few grammatical, spelling, or punctuation errors.	Many grammatical, spelling, or punctuation errors.

Exploring People and Cultures © Prufrock Press Inc.
Permission is granted to photocopy or reproduce this page for single classroom use only.

Lesson 19: Gathering Background Information on the Topic

Objective: Students will write notes on cards containing background information on their topics.

Materials:
- ○ Access to a library or media center
- ○ Note cards (index cards or teacher created)
- ○ Pencils
- ○ Thick rubber bands

Steps:
1. Take students to the library or media center to research background information on their cultural group. Before they begin, review with students the definition of primary and secondary sources.
2. Tell students how important it is to write good note cards. If they do a good job of writing note cards, then they will be able to sort and rearrange their notes without having to go back and look up the information, and they will have the bulk of the work done for their bibliography.
3. Have students write their name and their topic on the first card. Use the example in Figure 12 to show them how this should be done.

Name:_____

Topic: Artifacts of Cambodian Culture

Figure 12. Sample note card.

---

4. On the next card, students will write Source #1 in the top lefthand corner of the card. The source is where the information comes

from; the source number will change as students use different sources.

5. Students will then record the author of the source, the title of the book or article, the date and place of publication, and the page number(s) the student is using, especially if he or she is using a direct quote. If students are paraphrasing an author, they don't technically need page numbers. See Figure 13 for an example.

Source #1

Crew, L. (1989). *Children of the river*. New York, NY: Dell Publishing. Sundra fled Cambodia with her family to escape the Khmer Rouge army when she was 13. Four years later, she struggles to fit in at her high school in the United States.

Figure 13. Sample expanded note card.

---

6. The rest of the card can be used for information about the cultural group.

7. Students will use #1 on their cards until they change sources; they will then use #2 in the top lefthand corner (Null, 1998), and so on.

8. At the end of the research session, students will secure their note cards with a rubber band and keep the notes in their research notebooks.

9. After students have completed their background information, it will be time for them to complete their observations and interviews. When students transcribe their field notes, they need to remember to be as descriptive as possible so they may provide a vivid picture of their cultural group. Students will keep all of their field notes in their research notebooks.

Evaluation: Students successfully complete note cards with background information about their topic.

Lesson 20: Creating a Map of the Community

Objective: Students will create a visual representation of their research site.

Materials:
- ○ Drawing paper
- ○ Pencils
- ○ Colored markers

Steps:
1. Have students visualize the physical layout of the community they are studying. What are the major landmarks? Are there certain places that the people of the community congregate?
2. Students will then create a map of the community they are studying. Students will also make a key for their maps—this will help others read them.
3. After the maps are completed, students will spend some time reflecting on them to generate some ideas for their studies. Ask students, "If you could pick one area of the map that you thought exemplified the culture, what would it be?"
4. Students share their maps with a partner, explaining why they chose particular items to put in their maps.
   a. Have them share the one area they would choose to exemplify their culture.
   b. Invite some students to share with the whole class.
   c. Students will keep their maps with their data as an element of the research process. They can use their maps to help them write their final research reports.

Evaluation: Students create maps that provide adequate visual representations of their research sites.

Lesson 21: Writing a Description of an Area on the Map

Objective: Students will write a detailed description of a place on their maps.

Materials:
- ○ Completed community maps
- ○ Senses Graphic Organizer sheet, p. 81
- ○ Pencils
- ○ Paper

Steps:
1. Hand out the Senses Graphic Organizer sheet.
2. Have students choose a place they would like to describe on their community maps.
3. Have them close their eyes as you read aloud each section of the organizer (Overmeyer, 2005), and instruct them to think about how they could describe the chosen place using their senses.
4. After students have completed their graphic organizers, have them write a descriptive paragraph about the place they chose.
5. Have several students share their descriptions.

Evaluation: Students compose a descriptive paragraph that successfully paints a picture of the chosen area to the reader. An example of an excellent descriptive paragraph follows from *This House of Sky: Landscapes of the Western Mind* (Doig, 1973):

> It starts in the early mountain summer, far back among the high spilling slopes of the Bridger Range of southwestern Montana. The single sound is hidden water—the south fork of Sixteen Mile Creek diving down its willow-masked gulch. The stream flees north through the people-less land until, under the fir-dark flanks of Hatfield Mountain, a bow of meadow makes the riffled water curl wide to the west. At this interruption, a low rumple of the mountain knolls itself up watchfully, and atop it, like a sentry box over the frontier between the sly creek and the prodding meadow, perches our single-room herding cabin. (p. 3)

Picture books, such as Jane Yolen's *Owl Moon*, may provide additional examples of good descriptive writing for students.

Name: _____ Date:_____

Senses Graphic Organizer

SEE	HEAR
What does the place look like? What colors, textures, or shapes do you see? What words will help others see what you see?	What sounds do you hear? Are they high pitched or low pitched? Do the sounds overlap?

SMELL	TOUCH
What do you smell in this place? Is it sour or sweet? Is there more than one smell?	If you could touch different things in this area, what would they feel like? What words will help others to feel what you feel?

TASTE	FEEL
What tastes do you associate with this place? Have you eaten anything here that was really good? Have you eaten anything that you didn't like?	How does this place make you feel? Are you happy to be in this place? Are the other people in this place happy? Are they sad?

Exploring People and Cultures © Prufrock Press Inc.
Permission is granted to photocopy or reproduce this page for single classroom use only.

Lesson 22: Sorting Data

Objective: Students will sort their data based on patterns.

Materials:
- Ethnographic data
- Note cards
- Highlighters

Steps:
1. Have students take out all of their transcribed data. Provide each student with a stack of note cards. Students will be using a similar type of labeling on these note cards as they did on their library note cards.
2. The first step of the sorting process is for students to go through their data and highlight important parts. As students highlight their data, they will begin to see that some of the information is similar—these are the patterns in the data.
3. As students find patterns, they will label the top lefthand corner of a note card as Pattern #1 and state the pattern with some description or direct quotes to support the pattern. Additional field notes that support this pattern will be written on note cards with Pattern #1 written in the top lefthand corner
4. As students find new patterns, they will start another stack of note cards labeled in sequential pattern numbers. For example, the next card will be labeled Pattern #2. When students have completed their data sorting, they will secure their note cards with rubber bands and store them in their research notebooks.
5. This lesson might need to be repeated a few times before students find several patterns in their data. When students have found at least three patterns, then it is time to move on to Lesson 23.

Evaluation: Students successfully find at least three patterns during the data analysis process.

Lesson 23: Analyzing Data for Themes

Objective: Students will use critical thinking and problem solving to derive conclusions from their data.

Materials:
- Note cards
- Paper
- Pencils

Steps:
1. Data analysis of descriptive data consists of looking for patterns and themes observed in the data and using the critical thinking skills of synthesis and evaluation to decide what important themes need to be described. As Fetterman (1989) stated: "First and foremost, analysis is a test of the ethnographer's ability to think—to process information in a meaningful and useful manner" (p. 88). Students read through their data, analyzing their patterns to see if there are themes that may be derived from the data. Students might ask themselves the following questions:
   a. What are the data revealing?
   b. What are the strongest pattern(s) in the data?
   c. Is there a theme to this pattern?
   d. What conclusion may I draw?
   e. Does this conclusion tell me something about a behavior or attitude of people I am studying?

2. As students complete the analyzing activity, they will Think-Pair-Share with partners to decipher what their data are telling them. This will provide the students the opportunity to verbalize what they are thinking and make sure it is making sense to themselves and the other students.
3. Students might need more than one opportunity to look through their data for themes. After students have identified several themes, it is then time to move on to Lesson 24, clustering ideas.

Evaluation: Students successfully identify at least two themes in their data.

Lesson 24: Clustering Ideas

Objective: Students will cluster the themes and patterns generated from their research.

Materials:
- Blank note cards
- Note cards with themes and patterns
- Pencils
- Themes and Patterns Graphic Organizer sheet, p. 85

Steps:
1. Have students take out their data. Distribute the Themes and Patterns Graphic Organizer sheet on page 85. Students will identify the themes that have the most patterns, or evidence, in their data.
2. Have students put their research purpose or question on a note card and put it in the center of the graphic organizer.
3. Have students go through their note cards and find the themes that can be generated from the patterns they have found in their data. These themes will be placed around the research question or purpose.
4. Note cards with patterns will be grouped around the appropriate theme (Weiss, 1994).
5. After students have placed their themes and patterns around the question, they will look at the note cards with the background information about the subculture. Next, students will decide where this information will fit in with their data and place it around an appropriate theme. If the students' background information doesn't fit with a theme, then students may use it in the introductory paragraph of their papers.

Evaluation: Students are able to find several themes in their patterns of data.

Themes and Patterns Graphic Organizer

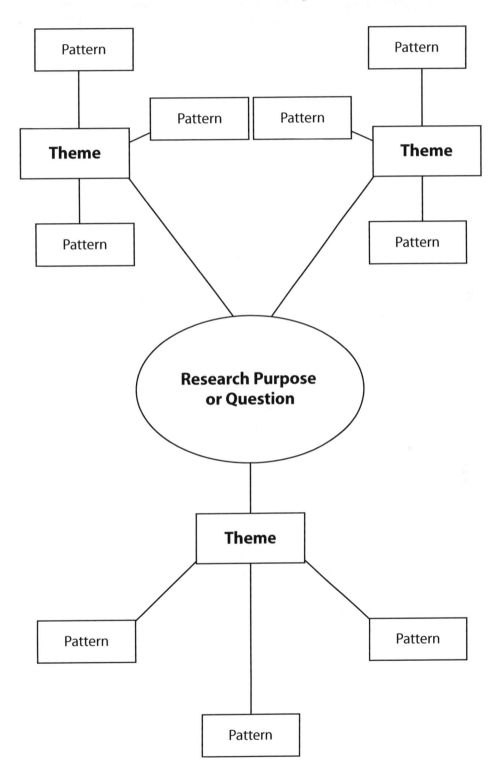

Exploring People and Cultures © Prufrock Press Inc.
Permission is granted to photocopy or reproduce this page for single classroom use only.

Lesson 25: Creating a Thesis Statement

Objective: Students will synthesize their data to create a thesis statement for their reports.

Materials:
- Completed Themes and Patterns Graphic Organizer sheet (see Lesson 24, p. 85)
- Data from mini-ethnography
- Pencils
- Paper

Steps:
1. The students took the first step to synthesize their data by organizing their themes and patterns using the graphic organizer. Next, they will summarize what they learned from identifying their themes and patterns. Using their completed Themes and Patterns Graphic Organizer sheets, students will write three strong paragraphs summarizing each of their themes.
2. After students write their summaries, have them Think-Pair-Share. Partners need to tell writers if the summary is not clear so writers can strengthen their summaries.
3. Students will now take their three paragraphs and synthesize their research by writing a statement that explains their personal response to their research: what they learned, why it is important, and how they think it adds to the knowledge about culture. Students will capture their thoughts in a single sentence. This sentence will be the thesis statement for their report. The students' themes and patterns will be the evidence that supports their thesis statements.
4. Give the students time to really think about their summaries and reflect on their research in order to write their thesis statements. Writing a good thesis statement is an invaluable skill that students will use throughout their school careers.

Evaluation: Students complete a well-written thesis statement.

Lesson 26: Outlining the Final Research Report

Objective: Students will create a graphic organizer that provides the direction for the final paper.

Materials:
- ○ Note cards of field notes, patterns, and themes
- ○ Before Outlining Your Research Report, Answer These Questions sheet, p. 88
- ○ Sample Outline of Research Paper sheet, p. 89
- ○ Paper
- ○ Thesis statement
- ○ Pencils

Steps:
1. The first step is to have students answer the questions using the graphic organizer on page 88:
   a. Who is my audience?
   b. What do I want readers to learn from this paper?
   c. What is my thesis statement?
   d. What is my hook? (How am I going to get readers interested in my paper?)
   e. What are my personal conclusions? (What did I learn from my research?)
   f. Do I have evidence to support my conclusions? (Are my conclusions supported by your data?)

2. After students have answered the five questions, it is time for them to format their information in an outline form. Outlining involves chunking information around individual subtopics. Students may have different ways to complete this task, including a formal outline, webbing, or concept mapping—but each student needs to create some type of outline.

Evaluation: Students successfully complete some type of outline or graphic organizer for their research reports.

Lesson 26 Worksheet

Before Outlining Your Research Report, Answer These Questions

Who is my audience?
What do I want readers to learn from this paper?
What is my thesis statement?
How will I get readers interested in my paper? (What is my hook?)
What are my conclusions? (What did I learn from my research?)
Do I have evidence to support my conclusions? (Do my conclusions match my data?)

Exploring People and Cultures © Prufrock Press Inc.
Permission is granted to photocopy or reproduce this page for single classroom use only.

Sample Outline of Research Paper

1. Outline of Research Paper
   a. Introduction
      i. Grab the reader's attention with a hook.
      ii. Introduce the topic (include your thesis statement).
      iii. Briefly summarize what you will present.

   b. Body Paragraphs
      i. Body Paragraph One: Information about your research process.
         1. Explain how you gathered your data and where you did your research.
         2. Give the number of observations, interviews, and surveys you completed.
         3. Provide any necessary background information your reader will need to understand your report (e.g., background information you found in your literature search).

      ii. Body Paragraphs Two and Three: Findings
         1. Discuss the themes you found in your data.
         2. Each theme needs to be supported by specific patterns from the data—use specific examples.
         3. Use descriptive language to paint a picture of the subculture for the reader.

   c. Conclusion
      i. Provide a brief summary of the main points.
      ii. Tell what you learned from doing the research.
      iii. Tell why the topic is important to you.
      iv. End with a strong sentence to make a lasting impression.

Exploring People and Cultures © Prufrock Press Inc.
Permission is granted to photocopy or reproduce this page for single classroom use only.

Lesson 27: Writing a Strong Lead

Note: This lesson was adapted from *Nonfiction Craft Lessons: Teaching Information Writing K-8,* by J. Portalupi and R. Fletcher, 2001, Portland, ME: Stenhouse Publishers. Copyright 2001 by Stenhouse Publishers. Adapted with permission.

Objective: Students will write a strong lead sentence to begin their reports.

Materials:
- Forms of Effective Leads sheet, p. 91
- Examples of strong leads from nonfiction magazines, nonfiction picture books, and newspapers
- Paper
- Pencils

Steps:
1. Explain to students that the first step in writing a good research report, or in any writing, is to develop a strong lead that will "hook" your audience and want them to read your report. Harvey (1998) cited William Zinsser, who said, "The most important sentence in any article is the first one. If it doesn't induce the reader to proceed to the second sentence, the article is dead" (p. 65).
2. Share some effective leads with students, and have them discuss why these leads grab the reader's attention and "hook" them into reading more of the piece.
3. Share with students the copies of the Forms of Effective Leads sheet on page 91. Have students get into pairs and talk about which of the leads might work for their writing.
4. Discuss the ideas as a class.
5. Have students draft some leads for their papers. Have them share their ideas in pairs.
6. Finally, students will choose the lead they feel is most effective to start their research report.

Evaluation: Students write effective leading sentences to begin their research reports.

Forms of Effective Leads

+ *News:* Tells the reader who, what, when, where, and why.

+ *Anecdote:* A brief story that reveals the essence of your subject.

+ *Quotation:* A quote lead may give additional authority and a fresh voice to the story.

+ *Descriptive:* Sets the scene for the story.

+ *Voice:* Establishes a tone for the story.

+ *Announcement:* Tells the reader what you are going to say.

+ *Tension:* Reveals the forces in the story and sets them in motion.

+ *Background:* Provides the background so the reader will understand the importance of the story.

+ *Historical:* Places the story in a historical context.

+ *Narrative:* Establishes the story as the form of the article.

+ *Question:* Involves the reader in the fundamental issue of the story.

+ *Point of View:* Establishes the position from which the reader will be shown the subject.

+ *Reader Identification:* Shows readers how the story relates to them.

+ *Face:* Gives the reader a person with whom to identify during the reading of the story.

+ *Scene:* Sets up an action between participants in the story that reveals the central meaning of the article.

+ *Dialogue:* Allows the story's meaning to come from the interaction of principal people in the story.

Note. Adapted with permission from *Writing to Deadline: The Journalist at Work,* by Donald M. Murray, 2000. Copyright 2000 by Donald M. Murray. Published by Heinemann, Portsmouth, NH. All rights reserved.

Exploring People and Cultures © Prufrock Press Inc.
Permission is granted to photocopy or reproduce this page for single classroom use only.

Lesson 28: Adding Quotations

Note: This lesson was adapted from *Nonfiction Craft Lessons: Teaching Information Writing K–8*, by J. Portalupi and R. Fletcher, 2001, Portland, ME: Stenhouse Publishers. Copyright 2001 by Stenhouse Publishers. Adapted with permission.

Objective: Students will add verbatim quotes to their research reports.

Materials:
   ○ Ethnographic reports
   ○ Field notes
   ○ Pencils

Steps:
   1. Read the students this excerpt from *The Denver Post* (Robles, 2011):

   A 13-year-old Aurora boy is recovering in the hospital after a rude awakening early Friday when a bear broke into his tent near Leadville and attacked him . . . The attack happened at 3:30 a.m. as Rick was camping with family members at a Colorado Bowhunter's Association event at Twin Lakes . . . The bear was going through a cooler in the campsite. It also checked out packages of bottled water and cartons containing about six dozen eggs . . . Rick escaped the attack with just a few bruises, scratches and a cut. He could be released from the hospital today. (p. B-2)

   2. Now, read students the excerpt again with the addition of a few verbatim quotes:

   A 13-year-old boy is recovering in the hospital after a rude awakening early Friday when a bear broke into his tent near Leadville and attacked him. The attack happened at 3:30 a.m. as Rick was camping with family members at a Colorado Bowhunter's Association event at Twin Lakes.
   Rick was in a tent when he woke to a noise outside. "I heard stuff just outside the tent," Rick said. "You know how bears snort?" The bear was going through a cooler in the campsite. "I didn't know what to do, so I just tried to say really still," Rick said. "I just didn't want to make it mad. But that didn't work." The bear became more vio-

lent, and sniffing turned into nibbling and biting. Rick said. "Luckily, my pajamas had been torn, so he just broke those off."

Randy Hampton, spokesman for the Colorado Parks and Wildlife, said that's when the bear was spooked. "The noise awakened other people—there were hundreds camping there—and they managed to scare the bear off," Hampton said.

Rick escaped the attack with just a few bruises, scratches and a cut.

"It's hard to understand you were so close to being dead," Rick said. (p. B-2)

3. Have students discuss which version of the story they found most compelling and which story gave them a better understanding of what happened.
4. Guide students to the conclusion that when you write, you need both the facts and some memorable quotes like those stated previously. Nothing is as powerful as the human voice. Adding verbatim quotes to their reports will bring their ethnographic studies alive.
5. Have students think about how quotes might strengthen their writing. Have them go through their pieces and add at least two verbatim quotes from their data.

Evaluation: Students successfully add at least two verbatim quotes to their ethnographic reports.

Lesson 29: A Strong Ending

Objective: Students will conclude their research reports with a strong ending.

Materials:
- ○ Ethnographic reports
- ○ Pencils

Steps:
1. In *To Kill a Mocking Bird* (Lee, 1960), the story begins with a discussion of Jem's broken arm: "When he was nearly thirteen, my brother Jem got his arm badly broken at the elbow" (p. 3). It ends on the night that arm is broken: "He [Atticus] turned out the light and went into Jem's room. He would be there all night, and he would be there when Jem waked up in the morning" (Lee, 1960, p. 323). The story tells of many events in the 320 intervening pages, but it starts and ends with Jem's arm. This is an example of a circular ending. This type of closure brings the piece full circle. One useful technique for helping writers with their concluding paragraph is to have them return to their thesis statement and reflect on it. Have students try a circular ending for their papers. Have them switch with a partner to share and discuss their endings.

2. Harvey (1998) suggested several questions for students to help them determine whether they have said all they want to say:
   a. Did I include all needed information?
   b. Did I tie up loose ends?
   c. Do I have anything I still burn to say?
   d. Did I answer my original questions?
   e. Will the reader feel satisfied or at least challenged?
   f. Does the ending fit? (p. 55)

3. Have students ask themselves the previous questions before concluding their reports. Have students help each other with suggestions for their conclusions.

Evaluation: Students write strong conclusions for their research reports.

Lesson 30: Editing the Research Report

Objective: Students will edit their own and a peer's ethnographic study.

Materials:
- Ethnographic reports
- Final Checklist sheet, p. 96
- Pencils

Steps:
1. Provide each student with a copy of the checklist for final editing. Students will go through the checklist to make sure they have completed all of the necessary pieces for their report. Any parts missing from the checklist will be added to the paper.
2. After each student completes the checklist, he or she will switch papers with another student and have this student also complete the checklist.
3. As students complete the process of editing each other's work, the final decisions for changes will be made by the author of the paper.

Evaluation: Students effectively complete the editing process on their own paper and a peer's paper.

Name: _____ Date:_____

Final Checklist

Me   Peer Reviewer

_____   _____   Does the paper have a good introductory paragraph? Does it have a hook? Does it provide a frame for the research?

_____   _____   Does the first body paragraph explain the different research methods the student used and how he or she selected his or her research site? Does it talk about the number of interviews and observations completed?

_____   _____   Does the second body paragraph present the findings and analyze/interpret the data collected?

_____   _____   Does the third body paragraph discuss the themes and patterns found in the data? Are the main points supported by specific examples?

_____   _____   Does the paper include at least two verbatim quotations?

_____   _____   Does the conclusion give a brief summary of what was covered in the report? Does it end with a strong sentence that makes a lasting impression?

_____   _____   Does each paragraph begin with a topic sentence?

_____   _____   Is the paper interesting? Has the author used good descriptive language and painted a picture of the setting and characters in the reader's mind?

_____   _____   If the author cited someone else, does he or she give that person credit?

_____   _____   If necessary, does the paper have a bibliography?

_____   _____   Are the spelling, grammar, and punctuation correct?

Exploring People and Cultures © Prufrock Press Inc.
Permission is granted to photocopy or reproduce this page for single classroom use only.

Chapter 5

Mini-Ethnographic Demonstration Fair

Sing your song, dance your dance, tell your tale.
—McCourt (2005, dedication)

Now that fieldwork is completed, organized, and written, the students and teacher will organize and implement a fair to demonstrate the learning of the completed mini-ethnographies. The fair's day, time, and length will be determined by the class, but it will be held at the most convenient time for students, parents, grandparents, friends, and other interested parties. A potluck dinner is always a possibility, because food often draws the most people. Choosing how to conduct the fair in your school is up to the teacher, the students, and other staff members.

The fair may be simple. As at a science fair, exhibits of each student's mini-ethnography may be displayed on inexpensive display boards with the student on hand to explain his or her project. However, the following plan would include an explanation and demonstration of ethnographic research. It would be presented and explained by the students. Lesson 31 includes suggestions for a student presentation.

Lesson 31: Mini-Ethnographic Demonstration Fair

Objective: Students will plan, create, and present key concepts about what they have learned through their completed field studies and mini-ethnographies.

Materials:
- Display boards
- PowerPoint software
- Photos of students at field studies and of student mini-ethnographies
- Student community maps (see Lesson 20)
- Computers for vodcasting, podcasting, and other technology applications
- What's the Same? What's Different? sheet, p. 100

Steps:
1. Students may complete the What's the Same? What's Different? sheet on page 100.
2. Students may suggest their own ideas for the mini-ethnographic demonstration fair. Ideas might include:
   a. **Group 1:** Design a 5-minute PowerPoint presentation (or Prezi or Glogster) with an explanation of ethnography and culture. Include an explanation of how ethnographies represent research, including the value of using ethnography for research. Include pictures of some or all of the class members' field study sites.
   b. **Group 2:** Recreate a field study experience. Possibly include a three-dimensional community map. Assign roles for student actors. Use a narrator to explain the research sequence.
   c. **Group 3:** Show how data were sorted and ideas clustered. Explain the importance of recognizing patterns and themes. Teach the group assembled for the fair by having them go through the process of organizing the ethnographies/field studies by categories (e.g., sports, clubs, church, family, pets, hobbies).
   d. **Group 4:** Each student will share the summary of his or her mini-ethnographic research in one single statement. Several or all students will discuss what cultural knowledge they gained and what benefit ethnographic research provided them.

3. Finally, allow time for all participants to circulate and view the research notebooks, display boards, and audio/video and hard-copy artifacts from the completed mini-ethnographies. Students may present additional products: vodcasts, podcasts, story-boards, digital stories, or other technology applications beyond the research notebook and completed written ethnography. See the Products List in Chapter 2 for ideas. Many technological applications exist for student demonstration of their mini-ethnographies. A simpler demonstration fair would use the KWL from Chapter 1 and then each student's mini-ethnography exhibit.

4. Students may share their ethnography with another student by completing the What's the Same? What's Different? sheet on page 100. Students will compare and contrast their ethnographic studies. Students may decide what criteria and rationale to use. Please take the time to analyze and synthesize student research projects, the highest of level Bloom's thinking. Students may post some of their technology applications on the class blog.

5. As a final activity to complete the ethnographic study, have students complete the L section of their KWL charts including learned vocabulary. Share students' answers to complete the classroom chart.

Evaluation: Students will complete at least one activity to demonstrate their learning and understanding of their mini-ethnography.

What's the Same? What's Different?

Name(s):_____

and _____

Compare and contrast your ethnographies. Choose three criteria to evaluate and discuss.

Comparison criteria and rationale	What's different?	What's the same?
Criteria: Why?		
Criteria: Why?		
Criteria: Why?		

Note. Adapted from *Q Tasks: The Student as Questioner*, by C. Koechlin and S. Zwann, 2006, Ontario, Canada: Pembroke Publishers. Copyright 2006 by Pembroke Publishers. Adapted with permission.

Exploring People and Cultures © Prufrock Press Inc.
Permission is granted to photocopy or reproduce this page for single classroom use only.

Conclusion

The Importance of Ethnographic Research

Upon completion of these ethnographic research and social skill exercises, students will have new insight and beginning skill levels at interpreting cultural traits in myriad research and social situations. Practicing and perfecting ethnographic skills will result in more successful experiences for students in grades 5–8 in the present and throughout their educational, work, and social lives. The exercises contained in this book will be the beginning of a lifetime of experiences for students interested in developing insightful interpersonal skills, resulting in intrapersonal awareness to be able to live and work with a variety of people.

References

Agar, M. H. (1986). *Speaking of ethnography*. Newbury Park, CA: Sage.

Agar, M. H. (1996). *The professional stranger*. New York, NY: Academic Press.

Anderson, G. (1990). *Fundamentals of educational research*. New York, NY: The Falmer Press.

Association for Supervision and Curriculum Development. (2008). *Educating students in a changing world: A position statement*. Retrieved from http://www.ascd.org/research-a-topic-/21st-century-skills-resources.aspx

Babbie, E. (1990). *Survey research methods* (2nd ed). Belmont, CA: Wadsworth.

Brown, A. (1995). *Organizational culture*. London, England: Pitman.

Burns, M. (2007). *About teaching mathematics: A K–8 resource* (3rd ed.). Sausalito, CA: Math Solutions Publications.

Caine, R., & Caine, G. (1991). *Making connections: Teaching and the human brain*. Alexandria, VA: Association for Supervision and Curriculum Development.

Colangelo, N., & Davis, G. A. (Eds.). (1991). *Handbook of gifted education*. Needham Heights, MA: Allyn and Bacon.

Creswell, J. W. (1994). *Research design: Qualitative and quantitative approaches*. Thousand Oaks, CA: Sage.

Doig, I. (1973). *This house of sky: Landscapes of the Western mind*. New York, NY: Harcourt.

Emerson, R. M., Fretz, R. I., & Shaw, L. L. (1995). *Writing ethnographic field notes*. Chicago, IL: University of Chicago Press.

Fetterman, D. N. (1989). *Ethnography step by step*. Newberry Park, CA: Sage.

Flake, C. L. (1992). Ethnography for teacher education. *Social Studies, 83*, 253.

Harvey, S. (1998). *Nonfiction matters: Reading, writing, and research in grades 3–8*. Portland, ME: Stenhouse.

Hittleman, D. R., & Simon, A. J. (1992). *Interpreting educational research: An introduction for consumers of research*. New York, NY: Macmillan.

Hofstede, G. J., Pedersen, P. B., & Hofstede, G. (2002). *Exploring culture: Exercises, stories and synthetic cultures.* Boston, MA: Intercultural Press.

Jackson, P. W., Boostrom, R. E., & Hansen, D. T. (1993). *The moral life of schools.* San Francisco, CA: Jossey-Bass.

Kingore, B. (2007). *Reaching all learners: Making differentiation work.* Austin, TX: Professional Associates.

Koechlin, C., & Zwaan, S. (2006). *Q tasks: The student as questioner.* Ontario, Canada: Pembroke.

Lee, H. (1960). *To kill a mockingbird.* Philadelphia, PA: J. B. Lippincott & Co.

Marzano, R. J. (1992). *A different kind of classroom: Teaching with the dimensions of learning.* Alexandria, VA: Association for Supervision and Curriculum Development.

McCourt, F. (2005). *Teacher man.* New York, NY: Scribner.

McKenzie, J. (1996). Making web meaning. *Educational Leadership, 54*(3), 30–32.

Murray, D. (2000). *Writing to deadline: The journalist at work.* Portsmouth, NH: Heinemann.

Null, K. C. (1998). *How to write a research report.* Westminster, CA: Teacher Created Resources.

Overmeyer, M. (2005). *When writing workshop isn't working: Answers to ten tough questions, grades 2–5.* Portland, ME: Stenhouse.

Overmeyer, M. (2009a). *What student writing teaches us: Formative assessment in the writing workshop.* Portland, ME: Stenhouse.

Overmeyer, M. (2009b). *Writing workshop.* Denver, CO: Temple Emanuel.

Petracca, M., & Sorapure, M. (2007). *Common culture: Reading and writing about American popular culture* (5th ed.). Upper Saddle River, NJ: Prentice Hall.

Piaget, J. (1954). *The construction of reality in the child.* New York, NY: Basic Books.

Portalupi, J., & Fletcher, R. (2001). *Nonfiction craft lessons: Teaching information writing K–8.* Portland, ME: Stenhouse.

Robles, Y. (2011, July 16). Bear put down after attacking Colorado teen at bowhunters event. *The Denver Post,* B-2.

Texas Education Agency. (2012). *Texas Essential Knowledge and Skills.* Retrieved from http://www.tea.state.tx.us/index2.aspx?id=6148

VanTassel-Baska, J., Feldhusen, J., Seeley, K., Wheatley, G., Silverman, L., & Foster, W. (Eds.). (1988). *Comprehensive curriculum for gifted learners.* Needham Heights, MA: Allyn & Bacon.

Vygotsky, L. S. (1978). *Mind in society.* Cambridge, MA: Harvard University Press.

Walker, B. (2000). *Curriculum jazz: The enactment of curriculum in a primary classroom.* (Unpublished doctoral dissertation). University of Denver, Denver, CO.

Winebrenner, S. (1992). *Teaching gifted kids in the regular classroom.* Minneapolis, MN: Free Spirit Press.

Weiss, R. S. (1994). *Learning from strangers: The art and method of qualitative interview studies.* New York, NY: The Free Press.

Wiggins, G., & McTighe, J. (1998). *Understanding by design.* Alexandria, VA: Association for Curriculum Supervision and Development.